ROTI

ROTI

90 simple recipes for the Indian
bread and its accompaniments

Anuradha Ravindranath

Contents

BAKE IN THE OVEN 108

FRY IN THE KADHAI 146

GETTING STARTED

The making of *Roti*

Roti kha kar jaana—if asked for a phrase that encapsulates the era I grew up in, I would quote this one. Unpretentious, earthy, and direct, as an invitation to "stay and eat with us," it captures the warm sociability of a time when hospitality resided in homes—gracious homes, big and small. It was where families and friends ate and celebrated together, where friends of friends were always welcome; where people stopped by to visit at all times of the day and were always expected to stay for a meal—not tea and cookies—but a meal. If you arrived late morning, you stayed for lunch, if you arrived early evening, then you stayed for dinner, and if it happened to be somewhere in between and you just could not stay that long, then the delicacies served often surpassed a meal.

I was born in 1953, just six years after India became an independent country. Our home was on 6 Aurangzeb Road in New Delhi and my earliest memories of it are of playing in its little garden with my father, and the family dog, Zulu. There was plenty of family on both my parents' side and people were in and out of our house all the time, lucky to be alive, and just glad to be together. I was very young, but I have strong memories of happy times as part of a small family. Another, somewhat hazy, memory leads me to believe that the exceptional quality of our dining table goes back to those days in the cottage. We had a cook named Sudama and, while I do not remember his daily fare, I can still taste the baked apples and caramel lace basket he used

to make. Even in the early 1960s, everything was still quite British—especially the food department of our home.

My father, whom we addressed as Bapu, was the great-grandson of Sir Gangaram, the renowned civil engineer and architect celebrated for his urban work in Lahore (in present-day Pakistan). Bapu grew up in undivided India, in a joint family in Lahore. His love for food and cooking, as I gathered from the stories he shared, developed from watching the cooks go about their daily business of preparing the most delicious meals for what must have been more than 20 to 25 family members, in addition to the large floating population of friends and work acquaintances. Bapu had a privileged view— the cook would lift and settle him securely on his shoulders whenever the little boy came into the kitchen. When Bapu turned 11, he was sent to Doon School, a boarding school in the foothills of the Siwaliks (in the present-day state of Uttarakhand in India). After completing his schooling, he returned to Lahore, where he finished college—it was a good life.

Politically, however, things were not going well. With independence came the partition of India in

Sudama with the author's brother Lakshman

The author's parents, Ranjit
and Kamala Rai in 1949

1947. Caught in the rioting that tore the
subcontinent apart, friends advised Bapu to
leave before the borders closed. Lahore was
not safe, no longer home. Friends and even
those considered extended family became
strangers and, like many others, he arrived
in Delhi with nothing in hand.

My mother's family was from Karachi,
also part of undivided India. Her progressive
and liberal father sent her to a university town
called Santiniketan, near Calcutta (now Kolkata)
in West Bengal, where his brother was a
higher-education teacher. On her return,
she taught at Ganga High School for girls in
Lahore. Despite skirmishes that hinted at the
violence that Partition might bring, she decided
to visit Delhi on August 14, 1947, to be there
at midnight when the first prime minister,
Jawaharlal Nehru, announced India's
independence. Expecting to be back in Lahore
shortly thereafter, all she brought with her was

an overnight bag. But, as rioting escalated
to carnage, the borders were sealed. There
was no going back—no option but to remain
in Delhi with the sister of a friend from
Santiniketan. She was 26 years old and,
though she lived to be 96, she never did
go back to the land of her birth.

Never one to sit idle if she could help it,
she volunteered to work at Kingsway Camp in
the old city of Delhi, one of the many camps
set up to house those displaced by Partition.
One day, when she had been delayed at the
camp, her friend arranged a car through a
family connection to take them home. My
father was driving the car. As it was past
curfew, the camp had provided them with
an armed guard. It did not occur to anyone to
ascertain if the gun was capped, and so when
my father had to brake abruptly, the gun went
off. The bullet went through my mother's arm.
With blood streaming and panic rising, she was

rushed to the already overflowing Wellington Hospital. Her arm was stitched up, without anesthesia, and she was kept in hospital for observation. My father visited every day and the rest, as they say, is history. They were married in 1949.

Even though they came from wealth, neither had very much at the time—what they did have was family. Bapu's aunt (his father's sister) was living in one of the spacious bungalows on Aurangzeb Road. She offered the newlyweds a little outhouse within the compound to set up home and start their life together. That is where I was born.

GETTING THE RIGHT INGREDIENTS

By the winter of 1957, we were well settled in "the cottage." Our beloved Zulu had died and to fill the gap, my brother and I took to feeding a stray, whom we named Jimmy.

Jimmy was wilful. However much we tried, he would eat his fill and go away. Bapu and I followed him one morning and found him trotting through the gates of the sprawling bungalow No. 3 on Prithviraj Road. It was obvious that the beautiful house was unoccupied. We wandered around until we spotted a chowkidar (a guard or watchman). One thing led to another and, in June 1958, Bapu raised enough money to buy the property from the owner, the Maharani of Tehri Garhwal. We moved in with Jimmy soon after.

No. 3 was a typical bungalow in the newly developed capital of New Delhi, designed by the British architect Sir Edwin Lutyens. The one-acre plot had lawns in the front and on both the sides. The walls were thick and retained heat in winter. In summer, the central open courtyard pushed the air to circulate freely through rooms that had plenty of windows and cooled the house down. There were no water heaters or air conditioners.

The kitchen too, did not have any fancy gadgets. Cooking was done on coal *chulhas* (traditional Indian stoves) set in brickwork. Since cooking was slow and went on for most of the day, they retained this heat throughout the day too. To take advantage of this, a cast iron box with a door was set in the middle. Surrounded by chulhas, it worked like an oven, in which it was possible to bake desserts. I particularly remember relishing the most delicious nan khatais (similar to shortbread)

The author with Jimmy and little Frosty in 1964

The author's childhood home
at No. 3, Prithviraj Road

that emerged from it. It was after we came to No. 3 that my father truly came into his own and took over the kitchen. This may have been due to the fact that my mother suffered a major loss of sensation in her arm from nerve damage caused by the shooting incident, which prevented her from taking on many domestic responsibilities. But that notwithstanding, what I do know for a fact is that Bapu enjoyed good food—discovering it, preparing it, and serving it.

As the years went by, I realized the importance of our dining table—how focal it was in building ties between family and friends. Every day there would be more than 8 to 10 members of the family sharing a meal, even though we were no longer a joint family. Various aunts and uncles, cousins of all ages and their friends, were urged *roti khake kar jana*. This was not just in our home. Hospitality came from the heart and was generously extended in all homes regardless of the size of kitchen or how well-to-do the family was.

THE PROCESS OF KNEADING

I was a sickly, cranky child who disliked eating and fussed about everything. I had to be begged, wheedled, and forced to even put a morsel in my mouth. Fortunately, Mai was there for me. She was from the hills of Himachal Pradesh and had made her home with us. Her name was Krishna but, though she was not old, everyone called her Mai (literally, "mother" but also used as a term of respect). She knew I fussed about everything related to food and had her own way of getting me to eat.

My father was passionate about growing uncommon vegetables and had planted many fruit trees as well as a grapevine. Much before leafy greens became a fad, our kitchen garden produced various kinds of *saag* (leafy green vegetables). Mai would take me around the garden to help her pluck whatever greens she could lay her hands on, including grape leaves, which I never imagined could be eaten. She would wash them before coarsely chopping them, while I watched fascinated. She would then take five or six handfuls of atta (whole wheat flour) in a *parat* (a steel basin often used in Indian kitchens to mix atta), add a pinch of salt and some water, then start kneading. In the blink of an eye, or so it seemed to me then, the dough was ready.

Next, a *kadhai* (Indian wok) would go on one *chulah* and a tava (Indian griddle for making rotis) on the other. She would pour mustard oil into the *kadhai*, followed by a couple of minced garlic cloves, chopped tomatoes, salt, turmeric— nothing was measured, it was all instinct—and finally the greens. Everything was stirred, covered, and left to cook as I watched transfixed.

She would then roll out the dough—it yielded no more than 4 rotis, almost 9in (22cm) in diameter and about ⅛in (2–3mm thick)—which she roasted on the tava. The cooking may have taken 20 to 25 minutes, but I was never bored. She spoke incessantly as she cooked, giving me all sorts of instructions that I still follow:

"Washing greens is important as the leaves have dust particles and who knows what's on them, even if you can't see them."
"Heat mustard oil but not until it smokes."
"Minced garlic releases aromas quickly."

She would place one, well-cooked roti, with ghee spread liberally over it, and a helping of greens on a plate for me and serve herself the same. We would sit on the floor by the kitchen doorway and as we ate, she would tell me about her life in the village. I, who did not like eating, would finish all that was on my plate without even noticing. This ritual lasted until I went to boarding school at the age of 11, and to this day, I can affirm that those were the best rotis I have ever eaten—flavorful and imbued with love, patience, and understanding.

Boarders—whether they like boarding school or not—learn to appreciate food as they are pretty much starving, or so it seems, throughout the day. I was away for only two and a half years, but the experience changed me. Once home, I started taking an interest in food, and not just in eating. I noticed how passionate my father was about cuisines from across India and the world, which he explored during his travels for work.

Every evening, after work, he would come home with bags full of ingredients for that day's experiment. I would watch him cook, listening as he imparted tips, just as Mai had done.

"The best result is when the ingredients are also of the purest quality."
"Ghee is most beneficial for health and perfect Indian food flavor."
"The best stock is homemade, both vegetarian and nonvegetarian."
"Herbs should always be used fresh."
"Rotis taste best when eaten hot off the tava."

RESTING AND ROLLING
Once I started paying attention, there was so much to notice—how the changing seasons influenced what was served at the table. The vegetables varied, as did the staple. As winter approached, everyone looked forward to sitting in the sun, enjoying bajre ki roti with makkhan (pearl millet flatbread with butter) or makki ki roti with sarson ka saag (cornmeal flatbread with mustard greens). These rotis were a major attraction and the kitchen seemed to produce a limitless supply.

The author with Mai just before her retirement in 1994

Winter brought with it a variety of parathas, possibly a nostalgic remnant of my father's Punjabi ancestry. The stuffed paratha ruled—traditional ones with aloo (potato), gobi–matar (cauliflower–peas), or mooli (daikon), as well as parathas with winter greens mixed in the flour. Our cook's paneer parathas, made with fresh, homemade paneer and kneaded into the dough with spices, tempted many friends to invite themselves over for a meal. While he loved a nice hot paratha, Bapu was a great advocate of a cold paratha (only one and made in pure ghee) and a bowl of any seasonal vegetables lightly sautéed with cumin, turmeric, and salt. This he maintained was the most balanced diet for lunch, "particularly in hot summer months."

As winter slowly turned to spring, Holi, the festival of colors, celebrated its arrival. The big, open courtyard where we ate winter lunch turned into a jamboree of people who were aunts and uncles of other people, nieces and nephews of other aunts and uncles, our parents' friends and their friends, and our friends and friends of those friends. My mother oversaw the kitchen and I think she enjoyed serving up a never-ending supply of food.

Samosas (fried pastries filled with spiced potatoes), gujias (sweet pastries), and, of course, the traditional bhang pakoras (fritters infused with cannabis leaves) started the day. Then, as the courtyard became a sea of colored water with not a face recognizable, puri-aloo would start arriving.

When the heat of summer crept up, roti and rice became the preferred staples. I remember sooji (semolina) roti with a little ghee being a particular favorite. It was served with tori-aloo (sponge gourd and potato curry), which made a perfect summer combination. Fruit replaced sweet desserts, with dozens of varieties of mangoes making the summer more tolerable. Aam ki launj (sweet and tangy mango chutney), aam panna (a drink made from raw mangoes), and my favorite, a slice of mango with a hot roti were especially cherished.

My paternal grandfather introduced me to this simple pleasure—he would roll a long sliver of ripe mango in a hot roti, spread a good amount of ghee, and eat it with a knife and fork—he often ate his rotis like that. I did not have much patience for the knife and fork, so I just ate it like a kathi roll (a wrap made with paratha, filled with a variety of ingredients). I still haven't understood why this absolutely delicious preparation doesn't find a place on any chef's table.

The monsoon brought with it relief from the intense, dry summer heat, and the heady fragrance of wet earth and fresh vegetation. Fried food sounded appealing again and puris were especially tempting—stuffed puris, such as bedmis; puris made with seasonal flours; or even simple atta and maida puris. They were eaten with classic pairings such as aloo ki sabzi (potato curry) or kaddu ki sabzi (pumpkin curry). No one could resist the combination of eating puri with hot halwa (a sweet dish). It was the season when a variety of cooked chutneys such as tomato, kamrak ki launj (star-fruit chutney), and karonde ki launj (Bengal-currant chutney) found their way to the table.

A bonfire night in the winter of 1978 (left) and the family enjoying lunch out in the sun, 1969 (right)

Cold puris also have their own unique place in my scrapbook of nostalgia. They had a very important place in train travel. Even today, an old-fashioned tiffin box remains amazingly evocative—of journeys with family, of puris, sukha aloo (dry potatoes), and achar (pickle) shared over 12 to 24 hours as the train click-clacked its way to our destination.

Another one of my favorite memories is of waking up early to drive to the railway station with my mother, even when we did not have a train to catch. We went to enjoy the hot puri-aloo that vendors cooked fresh at the station for early morning passengers. These puris always tasted extra special for some reason—it may have been the touch of adventure or the thrill of enjoying them amid the bustling chaos of a railway platform.

Bhaturas were the other fried speciality that we went out to eat. While puris and parathas were regularly made at home, bhaturas never were. The whole family would pile into the car and drive out to Bengali Market near Connaught Place in New Delhi. This was the place to enjoy street food, especially

puffed-up bhaturas served with a side of chhole (chickpea curry). Each bowl of chhole had one large piece of potato stuck in it and was garnished with chopped ginger and fresh coriander. What I have never understood is why bhaturas are served in pairs—though I must say I have no complaint with the addition at all.

Then the monsoon clouds made their way westward into the horizon, leaving behind the anticipation of the festival season. Dusshera, which commemorates the triumph of Lord Rama over Ravana, is preceded by nine days of fasting and feasting—fasting because only certain foods could be consumed and feasting because the alternative, fasting foods, the sweets, and the fruit, make up an entire cuisine category by itself. Each family has its own traditional specialities that have been fine-tuned over generations, and each one is exceptional.

On the tenth day, the kitchen would go into overdrive. More than 30 people would crowd around the table for the lunch. With food restrictions lifted, the table groaned under the weight of celebratory puris, aloo ki sabzi, kaddu ki sabzi, seasonal vegetables, raita (a yogurt-based condiment), halwa, and other sweets. As this was the first big meal for those who had been fasting, bingeing was expected.

Twenty days later comes Diwali, the festival of lights. The days were filled with visits to family and friends, card parties brightened the evenings, and it seemed the kitchen never shut down. Diwali brought with it the first nip in the air, announcing that winter was on its way.

THE WARMTH OF THE FIRE

The passing of time marked by the seasons was measured by the food we ate and shared. As I grew in age and experience, exposure to cultures and cuisines across India seemed to underline this reality. Wherever I went, I found the roti—not always a staple made of wheat as I was familiar with in North India, but made with other grains, even lentils, depending on what was grown locally. I was intrigued by the many variations I tasted.

Every region, and every home, rolled out rotis in different forms, with different grains and different methods of cooking, but in essence they were all the same—an expression of warmth and caring. The phrase *roti kha kar jana* was all about hospitality, straight from the heart, genuine, with no formality about it at all. I experienced it regardless of which part of the country I was in, an extension of another phrase often heard while growing up: *aap hi ka ghar hai,* or this is your home.

Over the years, closed doors have become the norm as noisy, gracious homes started giving way to silent, reserved flats and apartments, and joint to nuclear families. Technology has galloped at an unstoppable pace and the world has shrunk even further. World cuisines, fine dining, and fast food have come to be preferred over home-cooked food. This is not necessarily a bad thing: what I regret is the loss of individual flavors that our mothers and grandmothers imbued their food with, the loss of that heritage. I regret the reduction in the size of dining tables that leaves no place for guests. I regret the loss of a culture of hospitality at home. *Roti kha kar jana* just does not seem relevant any longer.

This book is my tribute to those times and an attempt to bridge the chasm by handing down a collection of recipes—just roti recipes. Those that I grew up with, as well as those that were so affectionately shared, ensuring that cooking at home and recipes that emerged and complemented it are not lost.

This compilation is not exhaustive—it could never be. All I hope is that it will bring friends together and will revive lost traditions. That it will inspire experimentation at home by generations to come, as well as by all those who have enjoyed a variety of Indian rotis and would like to try making them for themselves.

The leisurely warmth, bonhomie, and conviviality that blossoms around the dining table at home cannot be replicated. You can order in rotis but a reheated roti just does not taste the same. The best rotis are made and served hot from the home kitchen.

Types of flour

A variety of grains and lentils are grown across the vast expanse of India. Many of these are ground into flour and used to make rotis. While mechanical mills and commercial flour production have rendered the traditional chakki (hand-rotated grinding stones) almost obsolete, they can still be seen in some rural areas.

The word atta refers to flour, specifically whole wheat flour in northern India. It is ideal for making rotis due to its balanced bran content, which makes it easy to knead and handle. For flours made from other grains or lentils, specific names are used in combination with the term atta. These flours are often more coarsely ground and many are gluten-free. Since gluten-free flours can make the dough difficult to handle, a small amount of whole wheat flour or a binding agent, such as potato, may be sometimes mixed to improve its pliability.

Maida, or finely ground white flour, is highly refined with almost no bran. It is used to make deep-fried luchis (see pp162–163), as well as naans (see pp126–131) and kulchas (see pp120–123), which are popular fermented breads in India. Sooji, or semolina flour, made from durum wheat, when mixed with a small proportion of atta, also results in flavorful rotis. Bajre ka atta, or pearl millet flour, is predominantly produced in Rajasthan and enjoyed across northern India. Mixing a small amount of wheat flour with it helps to tone down its natural, slightly tart flavour. Ragi atta, or finger millet flour, is traditionally used in southern and eastern India. Jowar atta, or sorghum flour, once a staple in Karnataka, is now primarily used for special occasions and festivals.

Makki atta, maize (or corn) flour, is a winter flour popular in northern India. Besan or gram flour, made from split brown chickpeas, is common throughout the country. When combined with other flours, its versatile nature can give an interesting range of rotis and parathas. Kuttu atta, or buckwheat flour, is found in northern and eastern India and, like the seasonal fiber-rich singhare ka atta, or water-chestnut flour, is mostly eaten during traditional Hindu fasting periods when the consumption of grain is prohibited.

Many other flours such as chana dal atta, or split chickpea flour; moong chilka atta, or split green gram flour; and poha, or flattened-rice flour are used to produce a range of interesting breads. However, they are not stand-alone flours, as they cannot be kneaded to form a pliable dough.

Kitchen tools

Implements for making rotis are quite different from the usual kitchen tools. Not only is it important to have these at hand for the texture and taste of the finished product, but also because the process of roasting and frying requires quick and dexterous handling, which is made easier and safer, with the correct tools.

Tava Used for roasting bread, the traditional ones are heavy and made of iron, and can retain a more stable temperature. Today, terra-cotta and nonstick tavas are also popular. (A flat-bottomed frying pan or a crepe pan would also work).

Parat The traditional vessel in which dough was kneaded. It was flat and wide with raised sides to prevent spillage.

Jhaara/poni A perforated spoon with a long handle used for deep frying.

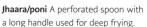

Palta A broad, flat, long-handled tool resembling a spatula, used to flip rotis and parathas on a hot tava.

Chimta Straight tongs used to hold rotis while puffing them up directly on the flame.

Kadhai A must in Indian kitchens, this is a heavy metal wok with a slightly broad base, designed specifically for deep frying.

Belan The rolling pin, which is almost always made of wood.

Chakla A flat circular slab of stone or wood on which rotis are rolled out. (A wooden cutting board used solely for this purpose could be used as an effective substitute.).

Accompaniments

Accompaniments and traditional pairings, some of which are timeless, are an integral part of Indian meals. Their ingredients are seasonal, fresh, and are often used raw to retain the maximum, natural food value.

RAITAS

In India, raitas are yogurt-based, savory dishes made with vegetables or a variety of greens, quite different from the sweet, fruit-flavored yogurts found in Western cuisine. Although some raitas are commonly paired with tandoori breads and meats—to complement the spicy main dishes with their cooling effect—there are no strict rules. For the best results, use fresh, high-quality vegetables and thick, well-set yogurt.

In Indian kitchens, roasted and ground cumin seeds are the most popular spices for flavoring raitas, with minced fresh cilantro and green chiles adding the final touch.

Experimenting with and adjusting the flavors in any raita recipe is certainly possible. However, aloo or potato paratha served with aloo raita might be less appealing unless you are a true aloo enthusiast. Vegetables, such as cucumber and onion release water, especially after adding salt. To avoid a watery raita, add the salt just before serving. Raitas can be stored in the refrigerator for about two days, except when they contain onions. Onion-based raitas should always be made and eaten fresh, as raw onions can develop an unpleasant odor over time, which affects the taste of the raita.

CHUTNEYS

Chutneys are quick, spicy, and flavorful sauces that can complement almost any meal. Although the recipes provided in this book are quite traditional, with a little imagination, a chutney can be conjured up from any number of everyday ingredients in the kitchen. Regional variations mean there is no one-size-fits-all rule, but chutneys typically align with seasonal ingredients—cooling cilantro and mint chutneys for summer, and spicier onion and garlic ones for winter.

It is important to note that chutneys are usually ground without adding water, which can dilute the flavor. The natural juices of the ingredients provide sufficient liquid content to allow grinding. Since most chutneys are uncooked, it is best to make small amounts to ensure they are consumed quickly—about two days in the refrigerator is the maximum they should be kept. Additionally, if raw onions are used, the chutney should not be stored at all.

ACHAR

In India, pickling means much more than merely extending the shelf life of food. Just like other accompaniments to food, pickles were developed predominantly to balance the digestive juices produced during eating, and to therefore aid digestion. Broadly, there are two traditional methods of pickling. The first one involves using oil, usually mustard and sesame oil, and pickles made in this way can be kept for up to a year. These oil-based pickles are prepared in two different ways. One way is to thoroughly coat the raw vegetables with salt and spices, place them in a ceramic or glass jar filled with oil, and leave the jar in the sun for the contents to ferment. It may take anywhere between one to two weeks for this kind of pickle to be ready to eat. However, it has a fairly long shelf life if it is kept in the refrigerator. The other oil-based method is to cook the vegetables in oil. Cooking the vegetables in this way results in a pickle that is ready to eat sooner, but it cannot be kept for too long.

The second method of pickling is more common in northern India, for fresh winter vegetables such as carrots, cauliflower, turnips, radishes, and beets. The vegetables are immersed in a water-based solution of ground yellow-mustard seeds, chiles, and salt, and then fermented in the sun. Once ready to eat, these pickles should be consumed within a week or two. Pickling in brine and vinegar, though now increasingly popular, was not a method traditionally used in India.

Northern India has another type of quick and simple pickle that is frequently prepared during the hot summer months. All that is needed is lemon juice and salt, in which ingredients such as freshly grated ginger, slices of lemon, and green chiles are immersed and left to ferment for a couple of days. Once ready, the pickle can be refrigerated for up to a week.

There are some pairings in Indian cuisine that no amount of fusion or innovation has ever been able to change, such as chana-bhatura *(see pp176–177)*, matra-kulcha *(see pp120–123)*, sarson ka saag-makki ki roti *(see pp46–49)*, dal-baati-churma *(see pp132–135)*, and aloo-puri *(see pp158–161)*. These traditional combinations, reiterated by the taste buds of generation after generation, are deservedly iconic—and that is how they are presented in this book.

DIY: White butter

Unsalted butter made by churning fresh cream

Ferment double cream in a covered bowl for two days until the cream begins to release water. Then use either a hand churner or electric whisk to churn the cream briskly until fat separates from the buttermilk as butter.

If needed, add 9½floz (280 ml) cold water or 8–10 ice cubes to help the butter solidify.

Gently transfer to a small bowl and store in the refrigerator.

DIY: Ghee

Indian clarified butter

Make white butter from 1¾ pints (1 liter) of double cream.

Place the butter in a heavy-based pan and simmer on a low heat until all the water has evaporated.

Ghee clarifies into a clear, pale, golden liquid, leaving small granules that settle at the bottom of the pan. Take care not to let these granules char, as that will ruin the ghee.

DIY: Yogurt

A dairy product obtained by coagulating milk

Warm 1¾ pints (1 liter) of milk (full-cream milk is preferable) in a heavy-based pan, but do not bring it to a boil.

Spread 1½oz (45g) of yogurt culture on the sides and bottom of a terra-cotta pot. A ceramic, glass, or steel bowl can also be used. Pour in the warm milk and stir for 1 minute.

Cover and set aside for 6 hours or until the yogurt is well formed. Slight warmth helps the yogurt set faster and better. On cold days, the milk should be slightly warmer and the bowl can be placed in a sunny spot or wrapped to retain heat as long as possible. Note that too much warmth will make the yogurt sour.

DIY: Paneer

Fresh, Indian soft cheese made from curdled milk

Bring 1¾ pints (1 liter) full-cream milk to a boil in a pan, then stir in 1½fl oz (45 ml) double cream, and bring to a boil again. Add 1½fl oz (45 ml) yogurt and stir until the milk curdles and the water separates from the casein. If this does not happen, add the juice of a medium-sized lemon. When the milk has curdled fully, strain in a colander lined with cheesecloth.

Fold the cloth to compress the paneer into a cube. Place this under a light weight, about 2¼lb (1kg), for 30 minutes to compact the cube of paneer further.

Unwrap and slice to use.

ROAST ON TAVA

Introduction

Eating a hot roti with butter or ghee is an almost sublime experience. It would be difficult to find anyone who disagrees with this statement. But, is there a standard, "typical" roti? The answer, quite obviously, is no. The roti is a non-fermented traditional Indian bread and, in a country as vast as India, every state, every town, every village, every household, in fact, has its own version of it. There can be many reasons for the difference —the type of flour used, or how much water is added to the dough, how long it is kneaded, how long it is left to breathe, is it rolled or patted out by hand, how thick or thin it is rolled out, is it finished on the tava or on the flame and, last but not the least, how much love has gone into its making.

Whole wheat flour is best for making an aromatic and tasty roti the traditional Indian way, though flour from different sources is likely to differ in both taste and texture. Whole wheat flour should be easily available, but if you aren't able to find it, look for a flour that is not highly refined, as a highly refined flour will make a dough that is sticky and pasty. On the other hand, the flour should not have a high bran content either, as it does not allow the dough to bind well, which will result in a roti that cracks easily.

Simple as it may be, water is essential to bind the dough. It may be necessary to make slight adjustments to the quantity given in recipes while kneading. Never pour in the water all at once—begin with a little and mix it in the flour, add some more, and collect all the flour into one crumbly whole. Start kneading, adding a little water at a time as you go along, until you have one compact dough ball that does not fall apart. It should not be too stiff or hard—if you think that it is, sprinkle a little more water. A good roti dough is soft and pliable.

After kneading, the dough must be kept aside for a minimum of 15 minutes. This allows the gluten to develop properly, increasing the overall elasticity of the dough, making it easier to roll out, and resulting in softer rotis. It is important to cover the dough when it is set aside—this is to prevent a crust forming on the surface as it dries out. This dry, grainy crust will hinder the smooth rolling of the roti and may cause it to tear.

Making dough balls is not just about portioning the dough. A perfect disk will make it easier to achieve a circular roti.

Making dough balls for individual rotis is not merely a matter of portioning the dough. The dough should be shaped into perfect spheres by applying gentle pressure as they are rolled between the palms, and then flattened to a disk. A perfect disk will make it easier to achieve a circular roti.

From here there are two basic ways to extend the disk to the required size. One is to use a rolling pin—it is awe-inspiring to watch the proficient roti-maker lightly wield a rolling pin as the dough disk, seemingly of its own volition, rotates slowly under it to extend into a perfect circle. As a beginner, it is fine to lift and turn the dough while rolling out the rotis to achieve the circular shape. While dry flour is needed to prevent the dough sticking to the work surface, keep in mind that the amount of dry flour used makes a difference—too much tends to dry out the roti.

The other method does not use a rolling pin at all. Instead, flatten and extend the ball of dough by pressing it between your palms. This is a common method in homes where thicker rotis are preferred. These handcrafted rotis are just as delicious, although there is a slight difference in the final texture as a rolling pin presses and packs the dough more tightly. The hand technique is also preferred for difficult-to-handle flours of other grains.

Rotis are best cooked on a tava (if you don't have a tava, use a flat-bottomed frying pan or a crepe pan). Always warm the tava on medium heat before placing the roti on it. A slight change in color is a sure signal that it is time to flip the roti. Having flipped it, watch for tiny blisters that form on the surface. Flip it again if they do not form, as these indicate that the roti is ready to face the flame. Remove the tava, turn up the flame, place the roti directly on it, and let it puff up.

While rotis are best served hot, modern lifestyles are not always conducive to such luxury. If not serving immediately, what works best is to spread some ghee—as much or as little as you are comfortable with—evenly between two rotis by rubbing them together. Then place the paired rotis in an insulated container with a paper napkin lining the base. When the rotis have cooled a little, cover them with another paper napkin and close the box. The paper napkins will absorb any moisture, preventing the rotis from getting soggy, and they will remain soft.

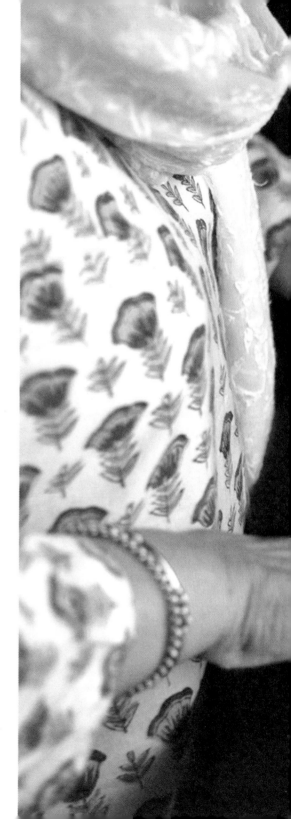

Rotis can also be stored in the refrigerator for about two days. They must be cooled, then kept in an airtight container, or wrapped in plastic wrap or foil. Reheat them on a tava on medium heat. If using a microwave, place them between two paper napkins in a covered dish for 30 seconds. They could also be reheated on medium heat in an air fryer.

While whole wheat flour is the primary flour used for rotis, one cannot overlook the large variety of rotis made of other grains eaten all over the country. Regional differences in the grains used were based on seasonal availability. Today, with modern storage facilities and transportation, the word "seasonal" is no longer relevant. Fresh, in-season flours are the best flours to use as they are without preservatives. If buying packaged flours, which are more easily available, it is important to check the production and use-by dates.

Over the years, experimentation in the kitchen and a constant desire for variation have given rise to two offshoots of the simple roti. One, by adding ingredients to the dough— dry spices, including salt, and minced fresh herbs. These can be added directly to the

flour and dry-mixed before kneading. Wet ingredients such as leafy greens and cooked lentils can also be added. These actually serve as the binder, in which case very little or almost no water is required while kneading. Ingredients such as fresh, non-set paneer can also be crumbled into the dry flour, and then kneaded while sprinkling water to make the dough. The one exception I have found is that fresh tomatoes cannot be added to the dough—they can be used only if cooked until all their water content is lost.

The second is the art of making a stuffed roti, which is specific to every household. To my mind, stuffed rotis may have started off as a "no waste" preference. Any leftover, cooked vegetables can be mashed and stuffed into a roti. The addition of minced fresh cilantro before mashing the leftover vegetables imparts a fresh flavor to these rotis. But, whether leftover or fresh, it is important that

the stuffing be dry and at room temperature. If it is warm or there is even a hint of water, the dough will not roll out. This is also why stuffed rotis are almost always made from whole wheat flour—the dough is pliable and lends itself to being stretched and pulled as required.

The following pages also give recipes for a range of different types of rotis from all over the country. Many use flours of other grains that are often difficult to knead and roll. While some of these are combined with wheat flour to promote elasticity and assist in binding, in others a binding agent may be used. Individual recipes for these seasonal and traditional rotis indicate how best to handle them.

While a roti may look simple, its making is anything but—do not get disheartened if your first attempt, second attempt, or even your third attempt ends up looks nothing like it should. The secret to making rotis is that practice makes perfect!

Phulka or Chapati

Everyone's favorite "roti"—a basic, flat, unleavened bread

Makes 6
Prep 40 minutes
Cook 15–20 minutes

9¾oz (280g) atta (whole wheat flour)
½fl oz (15ml) ghee or ½oz (15g)
    butter, for brushing

Set aside 1¼oz (35g) of atta on a plate and place the remaining atta in a deep bowl. Slowly add about 3½fl oz (105ml) of water, while kneading the atta into a pliable dough that does not stick to your hand or to the bowl. Cover with thin cheesecloth and let rest for 30 minutes.

Divide the dough into 6 equal portions and keep them covered while rolling the rotis, so the dough does not dry out. Take one portion and roll it into a smooth ball between your palms. Flatten the ball, turn it over in the plate of atta, and using a rolling pin, roll it out evenly to about 8in (20cm) in diameter.

Place a tava on medium heat, and wait until it warms before transferring the rolled-out dough onto it. Turn it over once or twice to roast both sides evenly. Take the tava off the heat and use a pair of tongs to place the roti on the direct flame to puff it up. Remove it quickly before it chars.

Alternatively, rotis can also be puffed up on the tava. After both sides are roasted, turn the heat to low. Wearing an oven glove, firmly but gently press down with your fingers while rotating the roti on the tava until it puffs up.

Brush with ghee or butter and serve hot.

Perfect when puffed up like a ball.

Sindhi roti

From Sind, a softer, richer version

Makes 6
Prep 40 minutes
Cook 20–25 minutes

9¾oz (280g) atta (whole wheat flour)
2fl oz (60ml) ghee

Reserve 1¼oz (35g) atta on a plate and place the rest in a deep bowl. Knead a pliable dough that does not stick to your hand or the bowl, by adding about 3½fl oz (105ml) of water in stages as required. Cover with thin cheesecloth and let rest for 30 minutes.

Divide the dough into 6 equal portions. Keep them covered while rolling the rotis, so that the dough does not dry out. Shape one portion into a smooth ball between your palms. Flatten it gently, turn it over in the plate of atta, and roll it out evenly to about 8in (20cm) in diameter.

Place a tava on medium heat and wait until it warms. Then, place the rolled-out dough on it and turn it over once or twice to roast both sides evenly. Reduce the heat and spread about 1 tsp ghee on the roti. Fold the roti in half and spread about ¼ tsp ghee on it. Fold it again into a quarter and spread about ¼ tsp ghee on the surface. Flip it and apply gentle pressure while spreading about ¼ tsp ghee on this side as well. Remove from tava and serve hot.

These rotis can be made earlier and kept in a warm box—they will remain soft.

Perfect when the roti has absorbed the ghee.

Do palli roti

Soft, light, almost paper-thin rotis, a treat for guests

Makes 12

Prep 1 hour 10 minutes

Cook 20–25 minutes

9¾oz (280g) atta (whole wheat flour)

8½oz (245g) maida (all-purpose flour)

1 tsp salt

1fl oz (30ml) vegetable oil

1fl oz (30ml) ghee

Once you have set aside 1¼oz (35g) of atta on a plate, place the remaining flours, salt, and oil in a deep bowl and mix well. Slowly add about 3½fl oz (105ml) of water, while kneading the flours into a pliable, nonsticky dough. Cover with a damp cloth and let rest for 1 hour.

Divide the dough into 12 equal portions. Cover them with thin cheesecloth while rolling the rotis, so the dough does not dry out. Take one portion and shape it into a smooth ball between your palms. Flatten it, turn it over in the plate of atta, and roll it out evenly to about 6in (15cm) in diameter. Repeat with another portion.

Spread ½ tsp ghee on one rolled-out roti, sprinkle with a little atta, and cover with the second rolled-out roti. Roll out the twin rotis to about 8–9in (20–23cm) in diameter.

Place a tava on medium heat. Once it is warm, transfer the twin rotis onto it. Turn them over once or twice to roast both sides evenly. Remove from tava, gently separate the rotis, and serve hot.

Perfect when the twin rotis can be easily separated.

Bhakri

A savory breakfast bread from Gujarat and Maharashtra

Makes 6

Prep 40 minutes

Cook 20–25 minutes

14¼oz (420g) atta (whole wheat flour)

1½ tsp salt

¼oz (10g) cumin, roasted and ground

1½oz (45g) fresh cilantro, minced

1½fl oz (45ml) ghee

Set aside 1¼oz (35g) of atta on a plate. Place the remaining atta in a deep bowl; add salt, cumin seeds, and fresh cilantro, and mix well. Then crumble the ghee into the atta. Slowly add about 4¾fl oz (140ml) of water, while kneading atta into a pliable dough that does not stick to your hand or to the bowl. Cover with thin cheesecloth and let rest for 30 minutes.

Divide the dough into 6 equal portions and keep them covered while rolling the rotis, so the dough does not dry out. Take one portion and roll it into a smooth ball between your palms. Flatten the ball, turn it over in the plate of atta, and using a rolling pin, roll it out evenly until it is about 6–7in (15–17cm) in diameter. Bhakri is slightly thick. Prick it lightly with a fork in 2–3 places.

Place a tava on medium heat and wait until it warms before transferring the rolled-out dough onto it. Allow the bhakri to get slightly roasted on both sides. Wearing an oven glove, firmly but gently press down with your fingers while rotating the bhakri on the tava, so that it roasts thoroughly. Turn it over once or twice to roast both sides evenly. Repeat the process until all the bhakris are ready.

Perfect when cooked to a pale golden brown.

Khamiri roti

A light, spongy, slightly tart bread from the Mughal era

Makes 6

Prep 40 minutes

Rest 6–7 hours

Cook 20–25 minutes

9¾oz (280g) atta (whole wheat flour)

1 tsp salt

1 tsp red chili powder

1 tsp carom seeds

½fl oz (15ml) ghee or ½oz (15g)
   butter, for brushing

Set aside 1¼oz (35g) of atta on a plate. Place the remaining atta and all the other ingredients in a deep bowl, and mix well. Slowly add about 3½fl oz (105ml) of water, while kneading the atta into a pliable dough that does not stick to your hand or to the bowl. Cover with thin cheesecloth and let rest for 6–7 hours so that it ferments naturally, then knead again.

Divide the dough into 6 equal portions. Make sure they remain covered while rolling the rotis, so the dough does not dry out. Take one portion and roll it into a smooth ball between your palms. Flatten the ball, turn it over in the plate of atta, and using a rolling pin, roll it out evenly to about 8in (20cm) in diameter.

Place a tava on medium heat, and wait until it warms before transferring the rolled-out dough onto it. Turn it over once or twice to roast both sides evenly. Take the tava off the heat, and use a pair of tongs to place the roti on the direct heat to puff it up. Remove it quickly before it chars. Brush with ghee or butter and serve hot.

Perfect when fluffy, soft, and chewy.

Ragi roti

Typical of the southern states, such as Karnataka and Andhra Pradesh

Makes 6

Prep 15 minutes

Cook 20–25 minutes

3¾oz (105g) atta (whole wheat flour)

7½oz (210g) ragi atta
  (finger millet flour)

1oz (30g) fresh cilantro, minced

1 tsp salt

1 green chile, minced (optional)

1fl oz (30ml) vegetable oil

1¼oz (35g) onion paste

½fl oz (15ml) ghee or ½oz (15g)
  butter, for brushing

Set aside about ¼oz (35g) of atta on a plate and place the remaining flours in a deep bowl. Mix in the fresh cilantro, salt, and green chile (if using). Add the oil and onion paste and mix well. Boil 3½fl oz (105ml) of water, pour it over the flours, and stir it in gently with a spoon. When the mix has cooled just enough to be handled (before it becomes cold), knead it to a soft and pliable dough that does not stick to your hand or to the bowl. Sprinkle a little more water, only if needed, to soften the dough.

Divide the dough into 6 equal portions. Remember to cover them with thin cheesecloth while rolling the rotis, so that the dough does not dry out. Shape one portion into a smooth ball between your palms. Flatten it, turn it over in the plate of atta, and roll it out evenly to about 6–7in (15–17cm) in diameter.

Place a tava on medium heat, and wait until it warms before placing the rolled-out dough onto it. Keep the heat low to medium, as this is a thick roti that needs time to cook. Turn it over once or twice to roast both sides evenly. Brush with butter or ghee and serve hot. Repeat the process until all the rotis are ready.

Perfect when brown and slightly crispy.

Lesu or Mandua ki roti

An interesting synergy of textures from Uttarakhand

Makes 6

Prep 25–30 minutes

Cook 20–25 minutes

12¼oz (350g) atta (whole wheat flour)

1½ tsp salt

7½oz (210g) ragi atta
   (finger millet flour)

1 tsp carom seeds

1 tsp red chili powder

1oz (30g) minced green cilantro

1fl oz (30ml) vegetable oil

½fl oz (15ml) ghee or ½oz
   (15g) butter, for brushing

Reserve about 1¼oz (35g) of atta on a plate; place the remaining atta in a deep bowl, add salt, and mix well. Slowly add 3½fl oz (105ml) of water, and make a pliable dough that does not stick to your hands or to the bowl. Cover with thin cheesecloth and let rest for 30 minutes.

Place the ragi atta in a deep bowl with the remaining ingredients. Bring 3½fl oz (105ml) of water to boil, pour it over the flour, and stir it in gently with a spoon. Wait until the mix cools just enough to be handled (it should not become cold) and knead it to a soft and pliable dough. Divide the dough into 6 equal portions. Keep them covered while rolling the rotis, so the dough does not dry out.

Take one portion of whole wheat dough and roll it into a smooth ball between your palms. Flatten it to about 4in (10cm) in diameter with your fingers. Place one portion of ragi dough in the center of the flattened dough, lift the edges to make a pouch, enclose it, and seal the ball of ragi in it. Flatten the pouch, turn it over in the plate of atta, and using a rolling pin, roll it out evenly to about 6–7 in (15cm–17cm) in diameter.

Place a tava on medium heat, and wait until it warms before transferring the rolled-out dough onto it. Turn it over and roast both sides evenly, until well done. Brush with butter or ghee and eat hot.

Perfect when the ragi filling comes as a surprise.

Makki ki roti, with sarson ka saag

A winter favorite from Punjab

Makes 6
Prep 10 minutes
Cook 15–20 minutes

8½oz (245g) makki atta (maize or
     corn flour)
2¼oz (70g atta) (whole wheat flour)
1 tsp salt
1 tsp red chili powder
2½fl oz (75ml) ghee

FOR SARSON KA SAAG

9¾oz (280g) sarson (mustard greens)
5oz (140g) palak (spinach leaves)
2¼oz (70g) bathua (goosefoot greens)
1¼oz (35g) methi (fenugreek greens)
1¼oz (35g) fresh cilantro
3–4 garlic cloves
2¼oz (70g) onion
2 whole red chiles
2 tsp salt
1oz (30g) besan (gram flour)

Mix both flours, salt, and red chili powder in a deep bowl.
Slowly add about 3½fl oz (105ml) of tepid water, to make
a pliable dough that does not stick to your hand or to the
bowl. Divide the dough into 6 equal portions. Cover them
with damp cheesecloth and let rest for 30 minutes.

Place a tava to warm on medium heat. Take one portion
of dough and shape it into a smooth ball between your
palms. Flatten it and pat it between your palms to flatten
it further. Moisten your palms to keep the dough from
sticking and continue patting it until the roti is about
6in (15cm) in diameter, then gently place it on the warm
tava. Turn it over a few times until the color lightens
and small golden-brown patches appear on the surface.
Spread ghee or butter on it and keep roasting for another
minute. Remove from tava. The makki ki roti should be
chewy with a light brown edge.

To make the saag, remove any thick stems from the
sarson and palak, and soak all the greens for 15 minutes.
Drain, wash in cold water, then place in a pressure
cooker. Add all the other saag ingredients, except the
gram flour. Pour in 9¾fl oz (280ml) of water, close the
lid, and bring to full pressure on medium heat. Then
reduce the heat and cook for another 15 minutes.
Set aside to cool.

For tempering

1fl oz (30ml) ghee

½ tsp asafoetida powder

1 whole red chile

1 tsp garlic, minced

1 tsp ginger, minced

1¼oz (35g) butter

Take the greens out of the cooker, and mash or blend in a food processor until smooth. Place them back in the pressure-cooker pan, add the cornmeal and ½oz (15g) of ghee, and cook on medium heat for 7–10 minutes without closing the lid. Stir every now and then so that the saag does not stick to the bottom of the pan.

Heat the ghee for tempering in a small pan, add the asafoetida powder and whole red chile. Stir and add the ginger and garlic. Roast until well done and smoky, then add it to the saag. Simmer for a minute or two.

Add a knob of butter, and serve hot with the makki ki roti.

Jolada rotti

Sorghum-based roti from Karnataka

Makes 6

Prep 15 minutes

Cook 20–25 minutes

2¼oz (70g) atta (whole wheat flour)

9¾oz (280g) jowar atta
   (sorghum flour)

1 tsp black pepper, coarsely ground

1 tsp cumin, roasted and ground

1 tsp salt

½fl oz (15ml) ghee or ½oz (15g)
   butter, for brushing

Having set aside 1¼oz (35g) atta on a plate, in a deep bowl, mix the remaining flours, black pepper, cumin seeds, and salt. Bring 3½fl oz (105ml) of water to boil, pour it over the flours, and stir it in gently with a spoon. Wait until the mix cools just enough to be handled (it should not become cold), then knead a soft and pliable dough that does not stick to your hands or to the bowl. If needed, sprinkle a little more water to soften the dough.

Divide the dough into 6 equal portions. Keep the dough covered with thin cheesecloth while rolling the rotis, so that it does not dry out. Take one portion and shape a smooth ball between the palms of your hands. Flatten it, turn it over in the plate of atta, and roll it out evenly to about 6–7in (15–17cm) in diameter.

Warm a tava on medium heat and transfer the rolled-out dough onto it. This roti is slightly thick, so keep the heat low to medium. Roast until the surface blisters, then flip it gently to roast the other side. Wearing an oven glove, firmly but gently press down with your fingers while rotating the roti on the tava so that it roasts thoroughly. Brush with ghee or butter, and serve hot.

Perfect when light brown and slightly crispy.

Bajre ki roti

From the semiarid regions of western India

Makes 6
Prep 25 minutes
Cook 15–20 minutes

7½oz (210g) bajra atta (pearl millet flour)
5oz (140g) atta (whole wheat flour)
1 tsp salt
½fl oz (15ml) ghee or ½oz (15g) butter, for brushing

Place both flours in a deep bowl, add the salt, and mix well. Slowly add about 3½fl oz (105ml) of tepid water, to make a pliable dough that does not stick to your hand or to the bowl. Cover with thin cheesecloth and keep aside for 15 minutes, then knead lightly again.

Divide the dough into 6 equal portions. Make sure the dough is covered while rolling the rotis, so that it does not dry out. Take one portion and roll it into a smooth ball between your palms. Flatten the ball and pat it between your palms to flatten it further. Moisten your palms to keep the dough from sticking, and continue patting it until the roti is about 6in (15cm) in diameter.

Place a tava on medium heat, and wait until it warms before transferring the rolled-out dough onto it. Turn it over a few times, until the color lightens and small brown patches appear on the surface. Spread ghee or butter, and continue to roast for a minute.

Perfect when soft and chewy.

PAIR IT WITH

LEHSUN-PYAAZ CHUTNEY

Grind 5oz (140g) onions, 1 garlic clove, 1-2 red chiles, 1 tsp salt, and 1 tsp lemon juice in a food processor without adding any water at all. If ground with a pestle and mortar, the result is an even more flavorful chutney.

Rumali roti

Thin to the point of being translucent like a rumaal—a handkerchief!

Makes 6

Prep 40 minutes

Cook 40 minutes

9¾oz (280g) atta (whole wheat flour)

5oz (140g) maida (all-purpose flour)

1 tsp salt

Set aside 1¼oz (35g) of atta on a plate. Place the remaining flours in a deep bowl, add salt, and mix well. Slowly add about 3½fl oz (105ml) of water, while kneading the flours into a pliable dough—this dough has to be a little sticky, so you may need to add a bit more water. Cover with a damp cloth and let rest for 30 minutes, then knead it again for a couple of minutes.

Divide the dough into 6 equal portions. Cover them with thin cheescloth while rolling the rotis, so the dough does not dry out. Take one portion and roll it into a smooth ball between your palms. Flatten the ball, turn it over in the plate of atta, and using a rolling pin, roll it out evenly until about 10in (25cm) in diameter—these rotis are almost paper thin.

Place a kadhai or a tava upside down on medium heat, and wait until it heats up. When a pinch of flour sprinkled on the inverted vessel turns golden, it has reached the correct temperature; drape the rolled-out dough on it. Turn it over once or twice to roast both sides evenly. Serve immediately, as these rotis do not store well.

Perfect when small, golden-brown blisters mark the surface.

Aloo ki roti

A classic, with a mouthwatering appeal for all ages

Makes 6
Prep 40 minutes
Cook 20–25 minutes

14¼oz (420g) atta (whole wheat flour)
½fl oz (15ml) ghee or ½oz (15g)
　　butter, for brushing

For stuffing
8¾oz (250g) potatoes
1½oz (45g) fresh cilantro, minced
1 tsp red chili powder
¼oz (10g) cumin seeds, roasted
　　and ground
1 tsp salt
2–3 green chiles,
　　minced (optional)

PAIR IT WITH

DHANIA-PUDINA CHUTNEY

Grind 5oz (140g) fresh
cilantro, ½oz (15g) mint
leaves, 1¼oz (35g) onions,
1¼oz (35g) tomatoes,
2 green chiles, and 1 tsp
of salt in a food processor
without adding any water
at all. Add 2 tsp lemon juice,
mix well, and serve.

Set aside 1¼oz (35g) of atta on a plate. Place the remaining atta in a deep bowl. Slowly add about 4¾fl oz (140ml) of water, while kneading the atta into a pliable dough that does not stick to your hand or to the bowl. Cover and let rest for 30 minutes.

Boil, cool, and peel the potatoes; crumble coarsely, then add all the other ingredients for the stuffing, and mash to a smooth consistency. Divide into 6 equal portions and set aside.

Divide the dough into 6 equal portions. Cover them with thin cheesecloth while rolling the rotis, so the dough does not dry out. Take one portion and roll it into a smooth ball between your palms. Flatten the ball, turn it over in the plate of atta, and using a rolling pin, roll it out evenly to about 4in (10cm) in diameter. Place one portion of the stuffing in the center of the roti, lift the edges to make a pouch, enclose the mix, and seal the dough pouch. Gently flatten the pouch, turn it over in the plate of atta, and roll it out, making sure to flip the sides at least once. Use a little dry atta to cover any potato stuffing if exposed.

Warm a tava and place the stuffed roti on it. Roast, turning it over once or twice. As soon as it browns, remove it, brush with ghee or butter, and serve hot.

Making rotis, especially stuffed rotis, can be daunting. To start, it may be better to make 2, almost full-size rotis. Spread the filling on one and cover it with the other. Press all around to seal the edges, roll gently with a rolling pin, and roast.

Perfect when it cooks to a nice, golden color.

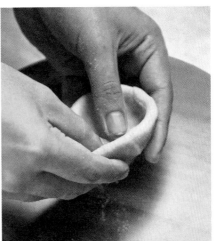

Matar bhari roti

Fresh, tender peas provide a zesty stuffing

Makes 6

Prep 1 hour

Cook 20–25 minutes

14¼oz (420g) atta (whole wheat flour)
½fl oz (15ml) ghee or ½oz (15g)
   butter, for brushing

For stuffing

9½oz (280g) peas, shelled
¼oz (10g) cumin seeds, roasted
   and ground
¼ tsp turmeric powder
½ tsp asafoetida powder
1 tsp red chili powder
1 tsp ginger paste
1oz (30g) fresh cilantro, minced
2–3 green chiles, minced
1½ tsp salt
1 tsp vegetable oil

Set aside 1¼oz (35g) of atta on a plate. Place the remaining atta in a deep bowl. Slowly add about 4¾fl oz (140ml) of water, while kneading the atta into a pliable dough, which does not stick to your hand or to the bowl. Cover and let rest for 30 minutes.

To make the peas stuffing, in a heavy-based pan, add all the ingredients and mix well. Add about 4¾fl oz (140ml) of water, cover, and cook on low heat, stirring once or twice until the peas are well cooked, and the water is completely absorbed. Remove from the heat, and mash well to a smooth consistency. Divide into 6 equal portions and cool.

Divide the dough into 6 equal portions. Cover them with thin cheesecloth while rolling the rotis, so the dough does not dry out. Take one portion and roll it into a smooth ball between your palms. Flatten the ball, turn it over in the plate of atta, and using a rolling pin, roll it out evenly to about 4in (10cm) in diameter. Place one portion of the stuffing in the center of the roti, lift the edges to make a pouch, enclose the mix, and seal it. Gently flatten the pouch, turn it over in the plate of atta, and roll it out, making sure to flip the sides at least once. Pat it with dry atta to cover any exposed peas stuffing.

Warm a tava and place the stuffed roti on it. Roast, turning it over once or twice. As soon as it browns, remove it, brush with ghee or butter, and serve hot.

Perfect when it cooks to a nice, golden color.

Gajar-Methi ki roti

An interesting variation of the stuffed roti, with crunchy carrots and greens

Makes 6
Prep 1 hour
Cook 20–25 minutes

14¼oz (420g) atta (whole wheat flour)
½fl oz (15ml) ghee or ½oz (15g)
   butter, for brushing

For stuffing
1 tsp vegetable oil
1 tsp cumin seeds
¼ tsp turmeric powder
¼oz (10g) red chili powder
1¼oz (35g) fenugreek leaves,
   finely chopped
9¾oz (280g) carrots, finely chopped
1oz (30g) fresh cilantro, minced
1½ tsp salt

Set aside 1¼oz (35g) of atta on a plate. Place the remaining atta in a deep bowl. Slowly add about 4¾fl oz (140ml) of water, while kneading the atta into a pliable dough, which does not stick to your hand or to the bowl. Cover and let rest for 30 minutes.

To make the carrot-fenugreek stuffing, heat the oil in a heavy-based pan. Add cumin seeds, turmeric, and chili powder; stir for a few seconds, then add the fenugreek leaves; stir, and add the carrots, fresh cilantro, and salt. Cover and cook until the carrots are soft, and there is no liquid in the pan at all. Allow to cool, then mash it to a smooth consistency. Divide into 6 equal portions, and cool before using them as stuffing for each roti.

Divide the dough into 6 equal portions. Cover them with thin cheesecloth while rolling the rotis, so the dough does not dry out. Take one portion and roll it into a smooth ball between your palms. Flatten the ball, turn it over in the plate of atta, and using a rolling pin, roll it out evenly to about 4in (10cm) in diameter. Place one portion of the stuffing in the center of the roti, lift the edges to make a pouch, enclose the mix, and seal it. Gently flatten the pouch, turn it over in the plate of atta, and roll it out, making sure to flip the sides at least once. Pat it with dry atta to cover any exposed stuffing.

Warm a tava and place the stuffed roti on it. Roast, turning it over once or twice. As soon as it browns, remove it, brush with ghee or butter, and serve hot.

Perfect when the discrete flavors can be tasted.

Paneer roti

Soft, flavorful, and hearty—this is a classic

Makes 6

Prep 1 hour

Cook 20–25 minutes

14¼oz (420g) atta (whole wheat flour)

½fl oz (15ml) ghee or ½oz (15g) butter, for brushing

For stuffing

7½oz (210g) paneer

1oz (30g) fresh cilantro, minced

¼oz (10g) red chili powder

¼oz (10g) cumin seeds, roasted and ground

1½ tsp salt

PAIR IT WITH

AAM KI LAUNJ

Take 9¾oz (280g) raw mangoes, peel, deseed, and cut like French fries. Sprinkle ¼oz (10g) of salt, and set aside for 1 hour, then drain. Heat ¼fl oz (10ml) oil in a heavy-based pan and add ¼oz (10g) panch phoran (*see p163*). When it splutters, add 2 whole red chiles, mango strips, ¼ tsp turmeric powder, and stir well. Add 2¼fl oz (70ml) of water, cover, and cook on medium heat until the mangoes are soft. Stir in 5oz (140g) sugar and cook until the mangoes take on a glazed appearance. Serve hot or cold.

Having set aside 1¼oz (35g) of atta on a plate, place the remaining atta in a deep bowl. Slowly add about 4¾fl oz (140ml) of water, while kneading the atta into a pliable dough that does not stick to your hand or to the bowl. Cover with thin cheesecloth and let rest for 30 minutes.

Place the paneer in a bowl; add the fresh cilantro, chili powder, cumin seeds, and salt, and mix until smooth. Divide it into 6 equal portions.

Divide the dough into 6 equal portions. Remember to keep it covered while rolling the rotis, so the dough does not dry out. Roll one portion into a smooth ball between your palms. Flatten the ball, turn it over in a plate of dry atta, and roll it out evenly to about 4in (10cm) in diameter.

Place a portion of the paneer mix in the center, lift the edges of the atta to make a pouch to enclose it, and seal the edges. Press gently to flatten it and roll it out to about 7in (18cm) in diameter, turning it on both sides and using a little dry atta to cover the paneer mix if it gets exposed.

Place a tava on medium heat, and wait until it warms before transferring the stuffed roti onto it. Turn it over once or twice to roast both sides evenly. Remove from tava as soon as it browns, and serve hot with ghee or butter. Repeat the process until all the rotis are ready.

Perfect when golden and crisp on the outside, soft on the inside.

Hari mirch and zeera roti

Spicy green chiles paired with cumin seeds adds a delightful zing

Makes 6
Prep 50 minutes
Cook 15–20 minutes

1¼oz (35g) fresh cilantro, minced

2–3 green chiles, minced

1 tsp cumin seeds

9¾oz (280g) atta (whole wheat flour)

1 tsp salt

1 tsp vegetable oil

½fl oz (15ml) ghee or ½oz (15g)
  butter, for brushing

Grind the fresh cilantro, green chiles, and cumin seeds together in a food processor.

Set aside 1¼oz (35g) of atta on a plate. Place the remaining atta in a deep bowl, then add the salt and cilantro-chile paste, and mix. Crumble the oil into the atta. Slowly add about 3½fl oz (105ml) of water, while kneading the atta into a pliable dough that does not stick to your hand or to the bowl. Cover with thin cheesecloth and let rest for 30 minutes.

Divide the dough into 6 equal portions. Keep the dough covered while rolling the rotis, so that it does not dry out. Take one portion and roll it into a smooth ball between your palms. Flatten the ball, turn it over in the plate of atta, and using a rolling pin, roll it out evenly to about 8in (20cm) in diameter.

Place a tava on medium heat, and wait until it warms before transferring the rolled-out dough onto it. Turn it over once or twice to roast both sides evenly. After both sides are roasted, turn the heat to low, and wearing an oven glove, gently but firmly press the roti with your fingers while rotating it on the tava. This will puff up the roti. Brush with ghee or butter, and serve hot.

Perfect when puffed up like a ball.

♦ PAIR IT WITH

ALOO KA RAITA

Take 5oz (140g) yogurt. Whisk in 1 tsp each of roasted and ground cumin, red chili powder, and salt. Add 1¼oz (35g) minced, fresh cilantro and 5oz (140g) boiled, peeled, and diced potatoes. Mix well and serve cold.

Missi roti

Gram flour or besan brings a nutty flavor to this North Indian winter favorite

Makes 6
Prep 25 minutes
Rest 1 hour
Cook 20–25 minutes

5oz (140g) atta (whole wheat flour)
5oz (140g) besan (gram flour)
1oz (30g) fresh cilantro, minced
1oz (30g) mint leaves, minced
1½ tsp black pepper, powdered
1 tsp cumin seeds, roasted and ground
1 tsp raw mango powder
1 tsp vegetable oil
1 tsp salt
½fl oz (15ml) ghee or ½oz (15g)
   butter, for brushing

PAIR IT WITH

KAMRAK KI LAUNJ

Heat ¼fl oz (10ml) vegetable oil in a heavy-based pan and add ¼oz (10g) of panch phoran (*see p163*). When it splutters, add 2 whole red chiles, 9¾oz (280g) star fruit cut in cross section, ¼ tsp turmeric powder, 1 tsp red chili powder, and 1½ tsp salt. Add 2¼fl oz (70ml) water, cover, and cook on medium heat until star fruit has reduced to half its quantity. Add 3½oz (105g) sugar and cook until star fruit looks glazed. Serve hot or cold.

Set aside 1¼oz (35g) of atta on a plate. Place the remaining atta in a deep bowl, add all the other ingredients, and mix. Slowly add about 3½fl oz (105ml) of water, while kneading the flours into a pliable dough that does not stick to your hand or to the bowl. Cover with thin cheesecloth and let rest for 1 hour.

Divide the dough into 6 equal portions, and keep them covered while rolling the rotis, so the dough does not dry out. Take one portion and roll it into a smooth ball between your palms. Flatten the ball, turn it over in the plate of atta, and using a rolling pin, roll it out evenly to about 8in (20cm) in diameter.

Place a tava on medium heat, and wait until it warms before transferring the rolled-out dough onto it. Turn it over once or twice to roast evenly on both sides, until light brown. Brush with ghee or butter. Repeat the process until all the rotis are ready. Serve hot.

Perfect when light brown and slightly crisp.

Palak ki roti

A very attractive, and delicious, green roti

Makes 6
Prep 1 hour
Cook 15–20 minutes

9¾oz (280g) spinach, finely chopped

2¼oz (70g) fresh cilantro, minced

2–3 green chiles, minced

1 tsp ginger paste

1 tsp garlic paste

½oz (15g) coriander powder

1 tsp cumin seeds, roasted
and ground

1 tsp salt

9¾oz (280g) atta (whole wheat flour)

½fl oz (15ml) ghee or ½oz (15g)
butter, for brushing

◆ **PAIR IT WITH**

KHATTA TAMATAR

Heat ¼fl oz (10ml) oil in a heavy-
based pan and add 1 tsp cumin
seeds. When they start to splutter,
add ½ tsp asafoetida powder,
1 tsp fennel seeds, ¼ tsp turmeric
powder, 1oz (30g) coriander
powder, 8½oz (245g) tomatoes
(cut into wedges), and 2 chopped
green chiles (optional). Cover
and cook on medium heat for 5
minutes. Add 4¾fl oz (140ml) water
and cook for 10 minutes. Remove
then sprinkle 1oz (30g) chopped
cilantro on top. Serve hot.

Wash and drain the spinach well and place it in a heavy-bottomed pan, together with fresh cilantro, green chiles, ginger paste, garlic paste, coriander powder, cumin seeds, and salt. Add about 2¼fl oz (70ml) of water and boil until the water dries out. Cool then blend into a smooth paste.

Set aside 1¼oz (35g) of atta on a plate. Place the remaining atta in a deep bowl, add the spinach paste, and mix it thoroughly. Slowly add about 1¼fl oz (35ml) of water, while kneading the atta into a pliable dough that does not stick to your hand or to the bowl. Cover with thin cheesecloth and let rest for 30 minutes.

Divide the dough into 6 equal portions and keep them covered while rolling the rotis, so the dough does not dry out. Take one portion and roll it into a smooth ball between your palms. Flatten the ball, turn it over in the plate of atta, and using a rolling pin, roll it out evenly to about 8in (20cm) in diameter.

Place a tava on medium heat, and wait until it warms before transferring the rolled-out dough onto it. Turn it over once or twice to roast both sides evenly. After both sides are roasted, turn the heat to low, and wearing an oven glove, gently but firmly press the roti with your fingers while rotating it on the tava. This will puff up the roti to a certain extent. Brush with ghee or butter, and serve hot.

Perfect when puffed up, and has brown spots.

Methi roti

Flatbread made with slightly bitter fenugreek leaves is a popular favorite

Makes 6

Prep 1 hour

Cook 15–20 minutes

9¾oz (280g) atta (whole wheat flour)

2¼oz (70g) fenugreek leaves, minced

1 tsp cumin seeds, roasted
   and ground

2–3 green chiles, minced (optional)

1oz (30g) fresh cilantro, minced

1 tsp salt

½fl oz (15ml) ghee or ½oz (15g)
   butter, for brushing

Set aside 1¼oz (35g) of atta on a plate. Place the remaining atta in a deep bowl, add the fenugreek leaves and all the other ingredients, including green chiles (if using), and mix well. Slowly add about 3½fl oz (105ml) of water, while kneading the atta into a pliable dough that does not stick to your hand or to the bowl. Cover with thin cheesecloth and let rest for 30 minutes.

Divide the dough into 6 equal portions. Remember to keep them covered while rolling the rotis, so the dough does not dry out. Take one portion and roll it into a smooth ball between your palms. Flatten the ball, turn it over in the plate of atta, and using a rolling pin, roll it out evenly to about 8in (20cm) in diameter.

Place a tava on medium heat, and wait until it warms before transferring the rolled-out dough onto it. Turn it over once or twice to roast both sides evenly. After both sides are roasted, turn the heat to low, and wearing an oven glove, firmly but gently press the roti with your fingers while rotating it on the tava. This will puff up the roti a little. Brush with ghee or butter, and serve hot.

Perfect when covered with small, crispy, brown spots.

Thalipeeth

Spiced multigrain flatbread from Maharashtra

Makes 6
Prep 30 minutes
Cook 20–25 minutes

5oz (140g) atta (whole wheat flour)

2¼oz (70g) jowar atta (sorghum flour)

2¼oz (70g) besan (gram flour)

½oz (15g) bajra atta
  (pearl millet flour)

½oz (15g) urad chilka atta
  (black gram flour)

½oz (15g) thick flattened rice or poha

1½ tsp ginger paste

½oz (15g) coriander powder

¼oz (10g) cumin seeds, roasted
  and ground

¼oz (10g) red chili powder

¼ tsp turmeric powder

2–3 green chiles, minced (optional)

2¼oz (70g) onion, minced

2¼oz (70g) fresh cilantro, minced

1½ tsp salt

1fl oz (30ml) vegetable oil

Set aside 1¼oz (350g) of atta on a plate. Place the remaining atta and all the other flours in a deep bowl, and mix well. Add the other ingredients, except the oil, and mix again. Slowly add about 4¾fl oz (140ml) of water, while kneading the flour into a pliable dough that does not stick to your hand or to the bowl. Cover with thin cheesecloth and let rest for 30 minutes.

Divide the dough into 6 equal portions and keep them covered while rolling the rotis, so the dough does not dry out. Cover the rolling surface with aluminum foil and brush the foil with a little oil. Take one portion and roll it into a smooth ball between your palms. Flatten the ball, turn it over in the plate of atta, and place it on the foil. Roll it out evenly with a rolling pin, until about 8in (20cm) in diameter. Cut a small, approximately ½in (2cm) hole in the center, to prevent the thalipeeth from puffing up.

Place a tava on medium heat and wait until it warms, then pour ½ tsp of oil onto it. Gently lift the foil and turn over the thalipeeth onto the hot tava. Remove the foil. Roast the thalipeeth evenly on both sides, adding another ½ tsp of oil for 3–4 minutes, until it develops golden-brown patches. Serve the thalipeeth hot, with accompaniments of pickle, raita *(see p20)*, or plain yogurt.

Perfect when golden brown with some darker, crispy patches.

Mung dal roti

The split green dal adds plant-based protein to this flatbread

Makes 6

Prep 40 minutes

Cook 20–25 minutes

9¾oz (280g) atta (whole wheat flour)

2 green chiles, minced (optional)

1oz (30g) fresh cilantro, minced

1 tsp ginger paste

¼oz (10g) cumin seeds, roasted and ground

5oz (140g) split green gram, cooked

½fl oz (15ml) ghee or ½oz (15g) butter, for brushing

Set aside 1¼oz (35g) of atta on a plate. Place the remaining atta in a deep bowl. Add green chiles (if using), fresh cilantro, ginger paste, and cumin seeds, and mix well. Since split green gram already has salt, there is no need to add more. Slowly add the split green gram, while kneading the atta into a pliable dough that does not stick to your hand or to the bowl. If required, add a little water. Cover with thin cheesecloth and let rest for 30 minutes.

Divide the dough into 6 equal portions. Make sure you keep them covered while rolling the rotis, so the dough does not dry out. Take one portion and roll it into a smooth ball between your palms. Flatten the ball, turn it over in the plate of atta, and using a rolling pin, roll it out evenly to about 8in (20cm) in diameter.

Place a tava on medium heat, and wait until it warms before transferring the rolled-out dough onto it. Turn it over once or twice to roast both sides evenly, until the roti turns golden brown. Brush with ghee or butter, and serve hot. Repeat the process until all the rotis are ready.

Perfect when a lovely golden brown in color.

PAIR IT WITH

DHANIYA-NARIYAL CHUTNEY

Grind 5oz (140g) fresh cilantro, 2¼oz (70g) grated fresh coconut, 1-2 green chiles (optional), 1 tsp salt, and ¼oz (10g) yogurt to a fine paste in a food processor, without adding any water at all. Do not use dried or green coconut—it is the flesh of the hard, brown, mature coconut that adds the flavor.

Lehsun ki roti

Spicy, with an extra aromatic edge of garlic

Makes 6

Prep 45 minutes

Cook 20–25 minutes

2 dry, whole red chillies (optional)

½oz (15g) garlic

1½ tsp salt

1oz (30g) yogurt

9¾oz (280g) atta (whole wheat flour)

½fl oz (15ml) ghee or ½oz (15g)
   butter, for brushing

If using whole red chiles, soak them for 1 hour and then drain well. Crush the garlic, red chiles , and salt together with a mortar and pestle, and add the yogurt to make a paste.

Set aside 1¼oz (35g) of atta on a plate. Place the remaining atta in a deep bowl and crumble in the garlic-chilli paste. Slowly add about 3½fl oz (105ml) of water, while kneading the atta into a pliable dough, which does not stick to your hand or to the bowl. If required, add a little water. Cover with thin cheesecloth and let rest for 30 minutes.

Divide the dough into 6 equal portions. Keep them covered while rolling the rotis, so the dough does not dry out. Take one portion and roll it into a smooth ball between your palms. Flatten the ball, turn it over in the plate of atta, and using a rolling pin, roll it out evenly to about 8in (20cm) in diameter.

Place a tava on medium heat, and wait until it warms before transferring the roti onto it. Turn it over once or twice to roast both sides evenly. Brush with ghee or butter, and serve hot.

Perfect when crisp and golden brown.

Gur ki roti

The sweetness of melted jaggery and fragrant fennel make a perfect combination

Makes 6

Prep 15 minutes

Cook 20–25 minutes

5oz (140g) jaggery powder

9¾oz (280g) atta (whole wheat flour)

½oz (15g) fennel seeds, crushed

½fl oz (15ml) ghee

½oz (15g) butter or ½fl oz (15ml)
    ghee, for brushing

Dissolve the jaggery in 4½fl oz (140ml) of warm water and set aside to cool.

Set aside 1¼oz (35g) of atta on a plate. Place the remaining atta in a deep bowl, add the fennel seeds, and crumble in the ghee. Slowly add the jaggery water, while kneading the atta into a pliable dough that does not stick to your hand or to the bowl. If required, add a little more water. Divide the dough into 6 equal portions. Remember to keep them covered with thin cheesecloth while rolling the rotis, so the dough does not dry out.

Take one portion and roll it into a smooth ball between your palms. Flatten the ball, turn it over in the plate of atta and, using a rolling pin, roll it out evenly to about 8in (20cm) in diameter. Place a tava on medium heat, and wait until it warms before transferring the rolled-out dough onto it. Turn it over once or twice to roast both sides evenly, making sure the roti does not stick to the tava. Brush with ghee or butter, and serve hot. Repeat the process until all the rotis are ready.

Perfect when golden brown and oozing jaggery.

Puran poli

A favored offering to the gods during the festival season in Maharashtra

Makes 6

Prep 3 hours 30 minutes

Cook 15–20 minutes

9¾oz (280g) atta (whole wheat flour)

2¼oz (70g) maida (all-purpose flour)

1fl oz (30ml) ghee

½ tsp salt

For stuffing

5oz (140g) split chickpea lentils

¼fl oz (10ml) ghee

¼ tsp nutmeg powder

1 tsp green cardamom powder

1 tsp fennel powder

1 tsp ginger powder

3½oz (105g) jaggery

Soak the split chickpea lentils for 3 hours. Then wash and drain before placing in a pressure cooker with about 9½fl oz (280ml) of water. Close the lid and bring to full pressure on medium heat. Leave to cook for another 5 minutes before removing. Set aside to cool.

Heat ¼fl oz (10ml) of ghee in a pan on low heat and add the dry spices. Stir for a few seconds. Add the cooked lentils and jaggery powder, and mix well—there should be very little water at this stage. Cook the mixture on low heat until it is absolutely dry. Set aside to cool.

Set aside 1¼oz (35g) of atta on a plate. Place the remaining flours in a deep bowl and crumble in 1fl oz (30ml) of ghee. Slowly add about 3½fl oz (105ml) of water, while kneading the flours into a pliable dough, which does not stick to the hand or to the bowl. Cover with thin cheesecloth and let rest for 30 minutes. When the mix has cooled, mash to a smooth consistency, divide into 6 equal portions, and set aside.

To make the poli, divide the dough into 6 equal portions. Cover them while rolling out the rotis, so that the dough does not dry out. Take one portion and roll it into a smooth ball between your palms. Flatten the ball, turn it over in the plate of atta, and with a rolling pin, roll it out evenly to about 4in (10cm) in diameter. Place one portion of the stuffing in the center, lift the edges to make a pouch, enclose the mix, and close it. Flatten it with the hand, then roll it out, as thinly as possible, turning it on both sides, and using a sprinkling of dry atta to cover any lentil mix if it is exposed.

Warm a tava and place the puran poli on it. Roast, turning it over once or twice while applying a little ghee, until it turns a golden brown. Serve hot or at room temperature.

Perfect when thin, soft and flaky.

Koki

A delectable, sweeter version of the savory flatbread from the Sindhi community

Makes 6

Prep 15 minutes

Cook 20–25 minutes

12¼oz (350g) atta (whole wheat flour)

3½fl oz (105ml) ghee

3½oz (105g) sugar

Reserve 1¼oz (35g) of atta on a plate and place the remaining atta in a deep bowl. Crumble 2fl oz (60ml) ghee and the sugar into the atta, and knead it into a stiff dough, adding just enough water to bind it.

Divide the dough into 6 equal portions. Cover them with thin cheesecloth while rolling the kokis, so the dough does not dry out. Flatten the ball, turn it over in the plate of atta, and using a rolling pin, roll it out evenly to about 4in (10cm) in diameter. Kokis are slightly thick. With a fork, lightly prick the surface of the koki in several places.

Place a tava on medium heat, and wait until it warms before transferring the rolled-out dough onto it. Spread ¾ tsp of ghee, turn it over, and spread another ¾ tsp of ghee. Roast both sides evenly, making sure the koki does not stick to the tava.

Repeat the process until all the kokis are ready. Serve hot, though they taste just as good when they have cooled.

Perfect when crisp, with a cookie-like texture.

ROAST ON TAVA WITH GHEE

Introduction

The paratha is a variant of the traditional roti—the difference lies in the application of ghee or oil between layers while rolling and while cooking on the tava. The health-conscious may use virgin oils and refuse to be as generous in their use, but the paratha remains a firm favorite that just has to be indulged in. What's more, it seems that in India, wherever you look, at every corner, be it a roadside vendor, dhaba on the highway, or restaurant, there is a paratha to tempt you. It is a great travel favorite—be it on the road, rail, or air, the paratha makes a regular appearance on the food tray. Today, the very popular kathi rolls (street-food wraps) are also often wrapped in thin parathas.

Unfortunately, in these health-conscious times, when "fat" has become a word synonymous with unhealthy, it has meant that parathas are looked upon by many as a harmful indulgence. This is a pity. Ultimately, the amount of fat used is in your hands. The recipes in this book give the optimum amount for a crisp paratha—it is a personal choice to use more or less. Some homes spread ghee between the layers and do away with it altogether while roasting on the tava—the result is a cross between a roti and a paratha, soft but not crisp. Others choose to use vegetable oils, olive oil, even margarine, instead of ghee. Whatever the method you chose, aficionados will tell you that unless cooked in ghee and served with a generous helping of butter, a paratha, stuffed, flavored, or plain, is not a paratha at all.

Just like the roti, parathas vary amazingly from household to household, even though the basic ingredients—that is, whole wheat flour, water, and ghee or oil—remain the same. The difference could be in the layering, or the shape—a square paratha with four layers, the triangular one with three—or perhaps, a pinch of salt added to the dough, or a little ghee to make the paratha even softer. This is just the plain paratha. When it comes to variations with more than just salt or ghee mixed in the dough, or stuffed parathas, there appears to be no end to the inventiveness. When adding

ingredients to the dough, the same rules apply for both rotis and parathas. The difference comes after the dough has been prepared, in the layering and cooking methods. For a really soft paratha, heat the tava on high initially, and then reduce the temperature before placing the paratha on it. Roasting on medium heat yields the best results. If the heat is too high, the parathas will become tough and hard. If the heat is too low, they will be undercooked, chewy, and soft.

Roasting on the tava with ghee or oil slows down fermentation, which is why parathas last longer than rotis. Be sure to let them cool before storing them in an insulated container, otherwise the trapped heat can release moisture and make the parathas soggy. If you are refrigerating them, use foil or parchment paper between each paratha to separate them, as the cooled-down ghee can cause them to stick to each other and make the layers flake off when one tries to separate them. Parathas can be reheated to original softness on the tava or in the microwave, much like rotis.

The stuffed paratha is an undisputed favorite for satisfying hunger pangs and taste buds at any time of day. Paired with plain yogurt, raita, or chutney, it becomes a complete, fulfilling meal. So, what should

> **Stuffed parathas are best eaten fresh.**
> **They do not store well and they cannot**
> **be reheated to their original crispness.**

you keep in mind while making a stuffed paratha? One of the most important aspects is the water content. For example, raw tomatoes, which have a high water content, cannot be added to a stuffing. Adding them can make the dough too sticky to handle, or cause the paratha to break or disintegrate while rolling, as the tomatoes may release water.

Since cooked vegetables usually contain salt, additional salt is generally unnecessary when using them as stuffing. If you prefer a saltier flavor, it is better to mix salt into the flour before kneading rather than adding it directly to the stuffing. For uncooked vegetables such as cauliflower, it is best to mince them, sprinkle with a little salt, and let them sit for 10 minutes. This process will release excess water, which can then be squeezed out by gently pressing the cauliflower in a colander.

The second crucial aspect of making a stuffed paratha is being able to achieve the correct texture. A beginner attempting to use a stuffing mix that is not smooth may find it easier to follow a different method. Roll out two plain rotis, spread the stuffing on one, and cover it with the other roti. Press the edges together to seal them, then gently roll out the stuffed paratha, applying minimal pressure. This will help flatten the paratha and make it easier to roast.

Stuffed parathas are best eaten fresh. They do not store well, especially if stuffed with precooked vegetables, and they cannot be reheated to their original crispness.

Flours of other grains and lentils can be used to make innovative parathas, whether mixed into the dough or used as stuffing. Such parathas are more commonly made in the eastern, western, and southern regions of India, where different types of flour are easily available.

In the state of Uttarakhand for example, the local legume gahat, also known as horse gram (*see p95*), which is very popular in the winter months, is also transformed into a stuffing for parathas. The sattu paratha (*see p98*), a well-known, popular breakfast food from eastern Uttar Pradesh and Bihar, traditionally used roasted flours of seven (*saat* therefore sattu) grains and pulses in the mix for the stuffing. Today, what is generally available and sold as sattu is the more easily available roasted-chickpea flour. This only underlines the infallible versatility of the very popular "anytime" favorite—the paratha.

Plain paratha

A basic roasted flatbread, which can liven up even the simplest meal

Makes 6

Prep 40 minutes

Cook 25–30 minutes

9¾oz (280g) atta (whole wheat flour)

2fl oz (60ml) ghee

Having set aside 1¼oz (35g) of atta on a plate, place the remaining atta in a deep bowl. Slowly add about 3½fl oz (105ml) of water, while kneading the atta into a pliable dough that does not stick to your hands or to the bowl. Cover with thin cheesecloth and let rest for 30 minutes.

Divide the dough into 6 equal portions. Keep them covered with thin cheesecloth while rolling the parathas, so the dough does not dry out. Take 1 portion and roll it into a smooth ball between your palms. Flatten the ball under your fingers, turn it over in the plate of atta, and using a rolling pin, roll it out evenly to about 6–7in (15–17cm) in diameter. Apply 1 tsp of ghee on the whole surface. Fold it in half, apply ½ tsp ghee, and fold it again to make a triangle. This gives the paratha its characteristic layers. Turn it over in the plate of atta, and roll it out once again to about 6–7in (15–17cm) equilaterally.

Place a tava on medium heat, and wait until it warms before transferring the rolled-out paratha onto it. Roast until the paratha starts to blister, then turn it over, and spread 1 tsp ghee on the surface. Turn it over again, and on this side, spread 1 tsp ghee. Flip it again. Roast both sides evenly until golden-brown patches indicate that the paratha is crisp and well cooked. Take it off the tava, and serve hot.

Perfect when crispy and golden brown.

PAIR IT WITH

GAJAR KA RAITA

Take 6¼oz (175g) of yogurt. Whisk in ¼oz (10g) roasted and ground cumin seeds and 1 tsp salt. Add 3½oz (105g) grated carrots, 1¼oz (35g) minced spring onions, 1¼oz (35g) minced fresh cilantro, 1oz (30g) roasted sesame seeds, and 2 minced green chiles (optional). Mix well and serve cold.

Lachha paratha

A layered paratha that just melts in the mouth

Makes 6

Prep 1 hour

Cook 25–30 minutes

9¾oz (280g) atta (whole wheat flour)

1 tsp salt

3fl oz (90ml) ghee

Reserve 1¼oz (35g) of atta on a plate, and place the remaining atta and the salt in a deep bowl and mix. Add about 3½fl oz (105ml) of water, while kneading the atta into a pliable dough that does not stick to your hands or to the bowl. Cover with thin cheesecloth and let rest for 30 minutes.

Divide the dough into 6 equal portions. Keep the dough covered while rolling the parathas, so that it does not dry out. Shape one portion to a smooth ball between your palms. Place it on the work surface, and start rolling with your hands to form a long rope of about 0.08in (2mm) thickness. Spread 1 tsp ghee on the inner surface and wind the rope into a 2-in (5-cm) coil. Flatten the coil, turn it over in the plate of atta, and roll it out evenly to about 6–7in (15–17cm) in diameter.

Place a tava on medium heat and wait until it warms, then transfer the rolled-out paratha onto it. Roast until the paratha starts to blister, then turn it over, and spread 1 tsp ghee on the surface. Turn it over and spread 1 tsp ghee on the other side. Roast both sides evenly, until golden-brown patches indicate that the paratha is crisp and well cooked. Remove from the tava, and serve hot.

Perfect when soft, flaky, and golden brown.

Malabar parotta, with pakke aam ki curry

Buttery paratha and mango curry, a mouthwatering combination from the state of Kerala

Makes 6

Prep 1 hour

Cook 25–30 minutes

17¼oz (490g) maida (all-purpose flour)

1 tsp sugar

¼oz (10g) salt

6fl oz (175ml) milk

3½fl oz (105ml) vegetable oil

FOR PAKKE AAM KI CURRY

1fl oz (30ml) vegetable oil

1 tsp cumin seeds

2–3 whole red chiles

2–3 sprigs of curry leaves

14¼oz (420g) ripe mangoes, peeled
  and cut into 2-in (5-cm) pieces
  (seeds to be saved)

1oz (30g) sugar

3½oz (105g) coconut powder

1 tsp red chili powder

Place the maida in a deep bowl, and mix in the sugar and salt. Slowly add milk, while kneading the maida into a pliable, nonsticky dough. Cover with thin cheesecloth and let rest for 15 minutes.

Knead the dough again for a couple of minutes, then divide it into 6 equal portions. Cover, and rest the dough for another 10 minutes. Take one portion, leave the others covered so that they do not dry out, and shape it into a smooth ball between your palms. Coat it with 1 tsp oil, then flatten it and roll it out to about 8in (20cm) in diameter. Apply 1 tsp of oil and continue rolling it out, to as thin as possible. Try rolling it evenly but do not worry about any holes if they appear.

Place a tava to warm on medium heat. Gather the rolled-out dough in accordion folds to form one long strip. Wind the strip into a coil, press down to flatten it, apply ½ tsp oil, and roll it out to about 6–7in (15–17cm) in diameter. Increase the heat, and transfer the parotta onto the tava. Roast until the parotta starts to blister, then turn it over, and spread ½ tsp oil on the surface. Turn it over and apply ½ tsp oil to the other side. Roast both sides evenly, until golden-brown patches indicate that the parotta is crisp and perfect. Remove it from the tava. Malabar parotta is well done when it is flaky and golden brown.

¼oz (10g) cumin seeds, roasted
and ground
½ tsp turmeric powder
¼oz (10g) salt

To make the pakke aam ki curry, heat the oil in a heavy-based pan, and add the cumin seeds, whole red chiles, and curry leaves. When they start to splutter, add the mango pieces and their seeds, the remaining dry spices, and salt. Cook until the mangoes are very soft—almost mushy—then add the sugar. As mangoes vary in sweetness, the key is to get the perfect balance of salt, sugar, and chile. Keep stirring until the sugar dissolves, then add the coconut powder, and leave to simmer for 2 minutes. Serve hot with Malabar parotta.

Mooli paratha

A spiced paratha stuffed with grated daikon for irresistible, tangy spiciness

Makes 6

Prep 40 minutes

Cook 25–30 minutes

12¼oz (350g) atta (whole wheat flour)

2fl oz (60ml) ghee

1 tsp salt

For stuffing

10oz (300g) daikon

1 tsp salt

1oz (30g) fresh cilantro, minced

¼oz (10g) red chili powder

¼oz (10g) cumin seeds, roasted
   and ground

¼oz (10g) raw mango powder

Peel the daikon and cut off the stem and tip. Wash and grate with a fine grater. Place the grated daikon in a bowl, add 1 tsp of salt, and set aside for 10 minutes.

Set aside 1¼oz (35g) of atta on a plate. Place the remaining atta in a deep bowl, add 1 tsp of salt, and mix well. Slowly add about 4¾fl oz (140ml) water, while kneading the atta into a pliable dough that does not stick to your hands or to the bowl. Cover with thin cheesecloth and let rest for 30 minutes. Squeeze the daikon to drain the excess water. Add the other ingredients for the stuffing, mix thoroughly, divide into 6 equal portions, and set aside.

To make the parathas, divide the dough into 6 equal portions. Remember to keep them covered while rolling the parathas, so the dough does not dry out. Take 1 portion and it roll into a smooth ball between your palms. Flatten the ball under your fingers, turn it over in the plate of atta, and using a rolling pin, roll it out evenly to about 5in (13cm) in diameter. Apply 1 tsp of ghee on the surface. Place one portion of the stuffing in the center of the rolled-out dough, lift the edges to make a pouch, enclose the mix, and seal the pouch. Gently flatten the pouch, turn it over in the plate of atta, and roll it out to about 7in (17cm) in diameter, making sure to flip and roll it on both sides. Use a little dry atta to cover any daikon mix, if exposed.

Place a tava on medium heat, and wait until it warms before transferring the rolled-out paratha onto it. Roast until the paratha starts to blister, then turn it over, and spread 1 tsp ghee on the surface. Turn it over and spread 1 tsp ghee on the other side. Flip it again. Roast both sides evenly until golden-brown patches indicate that the paratha is crisp and well cooked. Remove from the tava, and serve hot.

Perfect when a crisp casing reveals a soft and moist filling.

Aloo paratha

May be called the classic stuffed paratha, which has a spiced potato filling

Makes 6
Prep 45 minutes
Cook 25–30 minutes

12¼oz (350g) atta (whole wheat flour)
2fl oz (60ml) ghee

For stuffing
8¾ oz (250g) potatoes, boiled
1½ tsp red chili powder
¼oz (10g) cumin seeds, roasted
    and ground
¼oz (10g) raw mango powder
1½ tsp salt
1oz (30g) fresh cilantro, minced
¼oz (10g) fresh mint, minced

Peel and crumble the potatoes, add the dry spices, fresh cilantro, fresh mint, and salt, and mash to a smooth consistency. Divide the mix into 6 equal portions and set aside.

Set aside 1¼oz (35g) of atta on a plate. Place the remaining atta in a deep bowl, slowly add about 4¾fl oz (140ml) water, while kneading the atta into a pliable dough that does not stick to your hands or to the bowl. Cover with thin cheesecloth and let rest for 30 minutes.

Divide the dough into 6 equal portions. Keep them covered while rolling the parathas, so the dough does not dry out. Take 1 portion and roll it into a smooth ball between your palms. Flatten the ball under your fingers, turn it over in the plate of atta, and using a rolling pin, roll it out evenly to about 4in (10cm) in diameter. Place 1 portion of the stuffing in the center of the rolled-out dough, lift the edges to make a pouch, enclose the mix, and seal the pouch. Gently flatten the pouch, turn it over in the platter of atta, and roll it out to about 7in (17cm) in diameter, making sure to turn and roll it on both sides. Use a little dry atta to cover any mix if exposed.

Place a tava on medium heat, and wait until it warms before transferring the rolled-out paratha onto it. Roast until the paratha starts to blister, then turn it over, and spread 1 tsp ghee on the surface. Turn over and apply 1 tsp ghee to the other side. Flip it again. Roast both sides evenly until golden-brown patches indicate that the paratha is crisp and well cooked. Remove from the tava, and serve hot.

Perfect when crispy outside, with creamy, spicy aloo inside.

Gahat ki dal ka paratha

A local stuffed paratha from Uttarakhand with a horse gram filling

Makes 6
Prep 1 hour
Cook 25–30 minutes

12¼oz (350g) atta (whole wheat flour)
1 tsp salt
2fl oz (60ml) ghee

For stuffing
7½oz (210g) horse gram, washed
   and soaked overnight
3½oz (100g) onions, minced
3–4 garlic cloves
¼oz (10g) ginger paste
¼ tsp turmeric powder
¼oz (10g) red chili powder
1oz (30g) coriander powder
1 tsp asafoetida powder
1 tsp raw mango powder
1½ tsp salt
1oz (30g) fresh cilantro, minced

Drain the horse gram and place in a pressure cooker with all the stuffing ingredients. Add about 7½fl oz (210ml) water, bring to full pressure on medium heat, and cook for 15 more minutes. When cooled, drain excess water and mash well until smooth. Divide into 6 equal portions and set aside.

Reserve 1¼oz (35g) of atta on a plate, and place the remaining atta in a deep bowl and mix well. Slowly add about 4¾fl oz (140ml) water, while kneading the atta into a pliable dough that does not stick to your hands or to the bowl. Divide the dough into 6 equal portions. Cover with thin cheesecloth while rolling the parathas.

Take 1 portion and roll it into a smooth ball between your palms. Flatten the ball under your fingers, turn it over in the plate of atta, and using a rolling pin, roll it out to about 4in (10cm) in diameter. Place a portion of the horse gram mix in the center of the rolled-out dough, lift the edges to make a pouch, enclose the mix, and seal the pouch. Gently flatten it, turn it over in the plate of atta, and roll it out to about 7in (17cm) in diameter, making sure to turn and roll it on both sides. Use a little dry atta to cover any mix if exposed.

Place a tava on medium heat, and once warm, transfer the rolled-out paratha onto it. Roast until the paratha starts to blister, then turn it over, and spread 1 tsp ghee on the surface. Turn it over and spread 1 tsp ghee on the other side. Flip it again. Roast both sides evenly until golden-brown patches appear. Remove from the tava, and serve hot.

Perfect when dry and flaky inside.

Gobi paratha

A winter favorite, with a hearty filling of fresh, spiced cauliflower

Makes 6
Prep 40 minutes
Cook 25–30 minutes

12¼oz (350g) atta (whole wheat flour)
2fl oz (60ml) ghee

For stuffing
7½oz (210g) large cauliflower florets
1½ tsp salt
1oz (30g), fresh cilantro, minced
½oz (15g) fresh mint, minced
2–3 green chiles, minced (optional)
1 tsp cumin, roasted and ground
1 tsp ginger paste

Set aside 1¼oz (35g) of atta on a plate and place the remaining atta in a deep bowl. Slowly add about 4¾fl oz (140ml) water, while kneading the atta into a pliable dough that does not stick to your hands or to the bowl. Cover with thin cheesecloth and let rest for 30 minutes.

Wash and drain the cauliflower. Finely grate the florets. Add 1 tsp of salt and set aside for 15 minutes. Drain the grated cauliflower, and mix the remaining ingredients and salt into it. Rub in well to enhance the flavors. Then divide into 6 equal portions

To make the parathas, divide the dough into 12 equal portions. Cover them while rolling the parathas, so the dough does not dry out. Take 1 portion and roll it into a smooth ball between your palms. Flatten the ball under your fingers, turn it over in the plate of atta, and using a rolling pin, roll it out evenly to about 5in (13cm) in diameter. Repeat with another portion of the dough. Spread 1 portion of the cauliflower on one, and carefully cover it with the other rolled-out paratha. Press down on the edges to seal them. Gently roll it out to about 6–7in (15–17cm) in diameter, taking care not to break the dough.

Place a tava on medium heat, and wait until it warms before transferring the rolled-out paratha onto it. Roast until the paratha starts to blister, then turn it over, and spread 1 tsp ghee on the surface. Turn it over and spread 1 tsp ghee on the other side. Flip it again. Roast both sides, until golden-brown patches indicate that the paratha is crisp and well cooked. Remove from tava and serve hot.

Perfect when the cauliflower stuffing is soft and juicy.

Paneer paratha

Spicy and flavorful breakfast favorite

Makes 6
Prep 45 minutes
Cook 20–25 minutes

12¼oz (350g) atta (whole wheat flour)
2fl oz (60ml) ghee

For stuffing
7½oz (210g) paneer
1oz (30g) fresh cilantro, minced
2–3 green chiles, minced (optional)
¼oz (10g) cumin seeds, roasted
   and ground
1 tsp garam masala
1½ tsp salt

Set aside 1¼oz (35g) of atta on a plate and place the remaining atta in a deep bowl. Slowly add about 4¾fl oz (140ml) water, while kneading the atta into a pliable dough that does not stick to your hands or to the bowl. Cover with thin cheesecloth and let rest for 30 minutes.

Place the paneer in a bowl, add all the ingredients for the stuffing, and mix to a smooth consistency. Divide the mix into 6 equal portions and set aside.

To make the parathas, divide the dough into 6 equal portions. Remember to cover them while rolling the parathas, so the dough does not dry out. Take 1 portion and roll it into a smooth ball between your palms. Flatten the ball under your fingers, turn it over in the plate of atta, and using a rolling pin, roll it out evenly to about 4in (10cm) in diameter. Place one portion of the paneer mix in the center of the rolled-out dough, lift the edges to make a pouch, enclose the mix, and seal the dough pouch. Gently flatten the pouch, turn it over in the plate of atta, and roll it out to about 7in (17cm) in diameter, making sure to turn it on both sides. Use a little dry atta to cover any paneer mix if exposed.

Place a tava on medium heat, and after it warms, transfer the rolled-out paratha onto it. Roast until the paratha starts to blister, then turn it over, and spread 1 tsp ghee on the surface. Turn it over and spread 1 tsp ghee to the other side. Flip it again. Roast both sides evenly, until golden-brown patches appear. Take off the tava and serve hot.

Perfect when the moist filling perfectly complements the crisp casing.

Sattu paratha

The traditional breakfast specialty from the states of Bihar and Uttar Pradesh

Makes 6
Prep 45 minutes
Cook 25–30 minutes

12¼oz (350g) atta (whole wheat flour)
2fl oz (60ml) ghee
1 tsp salt

For stuffing

1½ tsp salt
7½oz (210g) onions, minced
7½oz (210g) sattu (roasted
   chickpea flour)
1½oz (45g) fresh coriander, minced
1½ tsp ginger paste
¼oz (10g) red chilli powder
¼oz (10g) cumin powder
1 tsp raw mango powder

PAIR IT WITH

NIMBU-ADRAK ACHAR

Place 5oz (140g) ginger either
julienned or grated coarsely, 2 green
chiles slit lengthwise, and ½oz (15g)
of salt in a clean and dry airtight
bottle. Add the juice of 6-8 lemons,
making sure the ginger is well
covered. Close the bottle, shake
to mix well, and set aside. In hot
weather, the pickle requires only
a day to be ready to eat, but when
it is cold it may take up to 3 days.

Rub a little salt into the onions to remove excess water
and set aside for 10 minutes.

Set aside 1¼oz (35g) of atta on a plate, and place the
remaining atta and salt in a deep bowl. Slowly add about
4¾fl oz (140ml) water, while kneading the atta into a pliable
dough, which does not stick to your hands or to the bowl.
Cover with thin cheesecloth and let rest for 30 minutes.

Drain and squeeze the onions, add the stuffing ingredients
and remaining salt, and mix well, to a sticky consistency.
Divide into 6 equal portions, cover, and set aside.

To make the parathas, divide the dough into 6 equal
portions. Cover them while rolling the parathas. Take
1 portion and roll it into a smooth ball between your
palms. Flatten the ball with your fingers, turn it over in
the plate of atta, and roll it out evenly to about 5in (13cm)
in diameter with a rolling pin. Brush the surface with 1 tsp
ghee. Place 1 portion of the sattu mix in the center, lift the
edges to make a pouch, enclose it, and seal. Gently flatten
the pouch, turn it over in the plate of sattu atta, and roll it
out to about 7in (17cm) in diameter, turning it on both sides.
Use a little dry atta to cover any sattu mix if exposed.

Place a tava on medium heat, and wait until it warms before
transferring the rolled-out paratha onto it. Roast until the
paratha starts to blister, then turn it over, and spread 1 tsp
ghee on the surface. Turn it over and spread 1 tsp ghee on
the other side. Flip it again. Roast both sides until golden-
brown patches appear. Remove from the tava and serve hot.

Perfect when the ghee is fully absorbed, resulting in a soft
and moist paratha.

Sidu

A stuffed, leavened bread from the state of Himachal Pradesh

Makes 6
Prep 1 hour
Rest 2–3 hours
Cook 1 hour 30 minutes

9¾oz (280g) atta (whole wheat flour)
¼oz (10g) dry yeast
1 tsp salt
1 tsp sugar
½fl oz (15ml) ghee

For stuffing
4¾oz (140g) walnuts, shelled
1 tsp ginger paste
1 tsp garlic paste
3½oz (100g) onions, chopped
2–3 green chiles, chopped (optional)

Add yeast and sugar in 2¼fl oz (70ml) of warm water, mix, and rest for 15 minutes.

Set aside 1¼oz (35g) atta on a plate. In a deep bowl, mix salt with the remaining atta, add the yeast mix, and slowly knead the atta into a pliable dough that does not stick to your hands or to the bowl. Cover and let rest until it doubles in size.

Grind the walnuts, ginger, garlic, onions, and green chillies (if using), without adding water, and set aside.

Divide the dough into 6 equal portions. Cover them with thin cheesecloth, so that they do not dry out while you are rolling the sidu. Take 1 portion and shape it into a smooth ball between your palms. Flatten it, and roll it out evenly to about 9in (23cm) in diameter. Spread 1½oz (45g) of the walnut mix on one side of the rolled-out dough. Fold the other side to cover the stuffing and press the edges to seal well. Make all 6 sidu.

Steam for about 15–20 minutes, or until a knife comes out clean after insertion into the side. Warm a tava on medium heat, spread ½ tsp of ghee on each side, and roast the steamed sidu for about 5–7 minutes, turning it over so that both sides turn a nice golden brown. Serve hot.

Perfect when a knife inserted comes out clean.

Anda paratha

A very popular street food in northern India, featuring a savory egg filling

Makes 6

Prep 45 minutes

Cook 25–30 minutes

12¼oz (350g) atta (whole wheat flour)

2fl oz (60ml) ghee

For stuffing

3 eggs

3½oz (100g) onions, minced

2–3 green chiles (optional)

1oz (30g) fresh cilantro, minced

½oz (15g) coriander powder

¼oz (10g) garam masala

1 tsp black pepper powder

1½ tsp salt

Set aside 1¼oz (35g) of atta on a plate. Place the remaining atta in a deep bowl and slowly add about 4¾fl oz (140ml) of water, while kneading the atta into a pliable, nonsticky dough. Cover and let rest for 30 minutes.

Crack the eggs into a bowl, beat well, mix in all the other stuffing ingredients, and set aside.

To make the parathas, divide the dough into 12 equal portions. Cover them with thin cheesecloth while rolling the parathas, so the dough does not dry out. Take 1 portion and shape it to a smooth ball between your palms. Flatten it, turn it over in the plate of atta, and roll it out evenly to about 6–7in (15–17cm) in diameter. Repeat with another portion of the dough.

Place a tava on medium heat, and wait until it warms before placing one rolled-out paratha on it. Allow the paratha to warm a little, then spread 2–3 tbsp of the egg mix evenly over the surface. Reduce the heat and cover with a lid for 30 seconds. Remove the lid and carefully place the second paratha on top of the first, pressing down on the edges to seal them. Spread 1 tsp ghee on the surface and cover again for a minute. Remove the lid, gently turn the parathas over, and spread 1 tsp ghee on the other side, and turn them over again. Roast both sides evenly, until golden-brown patches indicate that the paratha is crisp and well cooked. Remove from the tava and serve hot.

Perfect when the egg filling is light, fluffy, and fully set.

Keema paratha

A meat version starring minced chicken as the key ingredient

Makes 6
Prep: 1 hour
Cook: 25–30 minutes

12¼oz (350g) atta (whole wheat flour)
2fl oz (60ml) ghee

For stuffing
9¾oz (280g) chicken, minced
3½oz (100g) onion, minced
1oz (30g) ginger–garlic paste
¼ tsp turmeric powder
¼oz (10g) cumin seeds, roasted
   and ground
¼oz (10g) garam masala
½oz (15g) coriander powder
¼oz (10g) red chili powder
1½ tsp salt
1oz (30g) fresh cilantro, minced

PAIR IT WITH

PYAAZ-TAMATAR RAITA

Take 5oz (140g) yogurt. Whisk in 1 tsp each of red chili powder, roasted and ground cumin seeds, and salt, along with ¼ tsp of asafoetida powder (optional). Add 2¼oz (70g) each of minced tomatoes and onions, 1oz (30g) minced fresh cilantro, and 2 minced green chiles (optional). Mix well and serve cold.

Place all the ingredients for the stuffing, except the fresh cilantro, into a pressure cooker and mix well. Add 4¾fl oz (140ml) water, close the lid, bring to full pressure on medium heat, and leave to cook for another 15 minutes. Set aside to cool.

Reserve 1¼oz (35g) of atta on a plate; place the rest in a deep bowl. Add 4¾fl oz (140ml) water, while kneading the atta into a pliable dough, which does not stick to your hand or to the bowl. Cover and let rest for 30 minutes.

Open the pressure cooker and on low heat, dry out the minced chicken, almost to the point where it begins to stick. Transfer to a bowl, add the fresh cilantro, and mix well. When cooled, divide into 6 equal portions and set aside.

To make the paratha, divide the dough into 6 equal portions. Cover them with thin cheesecloth so the dough does not dry out. Take one portion and shape it into a smooth ball between your palms. Flatten it, turn it over in the plate of atta, and roll it out evenly to about 4in (10cm) in diameter. Place 1 portion of the mince mix in the center of the rolled-out dough, lift the edges to make a pouch, enclose the mix, and seal. Gently flatten the pouch, turn it over in the plate of atta, and roll it out to about 7in (17cm) in diameter, making sure to turn it on both sides. Dust any exposed mix with dry atta.

Place a tava on medium heat, and wait until it warms before transferring the rolled-out paratha on it. Roast until the paratha starts to blister, then turn it over, and spread 1 tsp ghee on the surface. Turn it over and spread 1 tsp ghee on the other side. Flip it again. Roast both sides evenly until golden-brown patches indicate that the paratha is crisp and well cooked. Remove from the tava and serve hot.

Perfect when   keema filling is soft inside a crisp parathra.

Virudhunagar parotta

A roasted and shallow-fried specialty from the city of Virudhunagar in Tamil Nadu

Makes 6
Prep 40 minutes
Cook 1 hour

9¾oz (280g) maida (all-purpose flour)
3½fl oz (105ml) vegetable oil
1 tsp salt

Set aside 1¼oz (35g) maida on a plate and place the remaining maida in a deep bowl. Add ½fl oz (15ml) vegetable oil and the salt, and mix well. Then slowly pour in about 3½fl oz (105ml) of water, while kneading the maida into a pliable dough that does not stick to your hands or to the bowl. Cover with thin cheesecloth and let rest for 30 minutes. Knead again and let rest for another 5 minutes. Divide the dough into 6 equal portions. Cover them while rolling the parathas, so the dough does not dry out.

Take 1 portion and roll it into a smooth ball between your palms. Flatten the ball under your fingers, turn it over in the plate of maida, and using a rolling pin, roll it out evenly and as thinly as possible. With your hands, roll the flat roti to form a long rope of about ⅛in (2mm) thickness. Coil this rope to make a spiral. Flatten the coil under your fingers, turn it over in the plate of maida, and using a rolling pin, roll it out to about 5in (13cm) in diameter.

Place a tava on medium heat, and wait until it warms before transferring the rolled-out paratha onto it. Half roast, turning it over once or twice. Remove from the tava and set aside. Repeat with the remaining portions until all the parathas are half-cooked. Heat the remaining oil on medium heat in a flat, heavy-based pan, taking care that it does not become smoking hot. Shallow fry until crisp and serve hot.

Perfect when lovely, deep golden brown, and crisp.

Meetha paratha

A sweet paratha that's a comforting favorite and a nostalgic childhood treat

Makes 6

Prep 40 minutes

Cook 40 minutes

9¾oz (280g) atta (whole wheat flour)

2fl oz (60ml) ghee

3oz (90g) sugar

Set aside 1¼oz (35g) atta on a plate, and in a deep bowl, knead the remaining atta into a pliable, nonsticky dough by slowly adding about 3½fl oz (105ml) of water in stages. Cover and let rest for 30 minutes.

Divide the dough into 6 equal portions. Cover them with thin cheesecloth while rolling the parathas, so the dough does not dry out. Shape 1 portion of the dough into a smooth ball between your palms. Flatten it, turn it over in the plate of atta, and roll it out evenly to about 6–7in (15–17cm) in diameter. Apply 1 tsp ghee on the whole surface. Sprinkle ½oz (15g) sugar over the paratha, pressing it in lightly with the rolling pin. Fold it in half, apply ½ tsp ghee, and fold it again to make a triangle, creating a layered effect. Turn it over in the plate of atta and roll it out once again to about 6–7in (15–17cm) equilaterally.

Place a tava on medium heat, and wait until it warms before placing the rolled-out paratha onto it. Roast until the paratha starts to blister, then turn it over, and spread 1 tsp ghee on the surface. Turn it over and spread 1 tsp ghee on the other side. Flip it again. Roast both sides evenly, taking care not to burn the sugar, until golden-brown patches indicate that the paratha is crisp and well cooked. Remove from the tava and serve hot.

Perfect when crispy, golden-brown outside with melted sugar inside.

BAKE IN
THE OVEN

Introduction

The most popular Indian fermented breads are kulchas and naans. Unlike rotis and parathas, which are primarily made with whole wheat flour, these are made from refined (all-purpose) flour. Moreover, these fermented breads were traditionally baked in the tandoor.

There was a time when the tandoor had a place in many kitchens of northern India—the urban metropolis of Delhi was no exception. Those residential areas that did not have a tandoor could still get freshly baked tandoori breads. For a small fee, a woman would come around every day and take the required dough from each household. She would then bake the specified breads in her tandoor and deliver them.

Not only does the modern kitchen rarely have place for a coal-fired tandoor, today access to a tandoor has also become a thing of the past. Fortunately, it is possible to bake these breads at home in the oven. The basic method remains the same, with the only significant loss being the smoky flavor imparted by an open fire. The kulcha can also be made on the tava, as detailed in this section.

Since refined flour is being used, the dough has to be kneaded well, until it no longer sticks to the hand. After kneading the dough, it must be set aside to ferment—for how long depends on the ambient temperature, but indicative times are mentioned in the recipes. In cooler conditions, covering the dough with a warm cloth will help in fermentation.

The inclusion of oil or butter in the dough should prevent it from sticking while rolling. If it does stick, the work surface can be lightly dusted with dry flour. After rolling out the dough, the process of baking in the oven is similar to that of baking in a tandoor. The side of the bread that will come in contact with the baking pan of the oven must be moistened before being put in. Except for some of the thicker, special breads, turning over to ensure even cooking is not needed as both sides cook simultaneously. The ideal oven temperatures are mentioned in each

At home, and without a tandoor, it is possible to bake these breads in the oven, with the only significant loss being the smoky flavor imparted by an open fire.

recipe. It is important to know that the microwave is not suitable for this type of cooking.

Fermented breads can also be made with ingredients in the dough, or stuffed, in much the same way as rotis and parathas. However, other than the plain kulcha, these breads cannot be reheated. Whether on the tava or in the oven, reheating destroys their flavor and texture, making them almost too tough to chew.

Of all Indian breads, it is, perhaps, the kulcha that is least known outside the subcontinent. Usually eaten with chana (*see pp176–177*) or matra (*see p121*), it is very popular in North India and, as with other breads, its popularity has led to many innovations. Until recently, the kulcha was a flat and light bread, neither very thick nor fluffy. While street-food stalls still serve the traditional flat kulcha, fluffy kulchas with a whole range of toppings can now be seen

in many bakeries, competing with the variety of breads available. Stuffed kulchas are also a recent addition, with potato and split-chickpea lentil fillings being the favorites.

Plain kulchas can be stored the same way as you would parathas. They can be kept in the fridge for up to two days. The best way to reheat them is in the microwave. Place a paper napkin in a microwave dish. Take a couple of kulchas—do not heat too many at one time—sprinkle a few drops of water between each, place another paper napkin on top, then cover with a microwave-suitable lid, and heat for one minute. Let them rest for a minute or so before serving. Stuffed kulchas do not store well.

The naan, which has quietly held its own for at least 600 years, is perhaps the most widely known and popular tandoori bread. This is not to say it has not undergone changes. Though the tandoor may have lost its place in the larger domestic framework, there are many chefs who study its concepts and master the technique of cooking in it, producing an unlimited variety of the most innovative and soul-satisfying breads. In addition, the visual thrill of watching an expert tandoori cook in action has secured the tandoor's place in today's "open kitchen" restaurants.

While the classic naan, with its traditional pairing of vegetarian and meat curries, still stands firm in its position as leading favorite, a variety of stuffed naans have become mainstream and are in great demand. As with rotis and parathas, any cooked vegetable or a mince of chicken or lamb can be used as stuffing for naans. Sprinkling chopped fresh mint, sesame seeds, nigella seeds, melon seeds, fresh cilantro, ginger slivers, green chiles, and so on, on top, just before baking, greatly enhances the

flavors. Be sure to remember that using tomato or any watery vegetable as stuffing is an absolute no.

In addition to these better-known examples, different parts of the country bake their own unique breads. For example, of the many baked in the northern region of Kashmir, the lavasa (*see pp124–125*), an everyday fermented flatbread, slightly resembles the kulcha. The tsot (*see pp136–137*), a small, cookie-like bread, about 4–5in (10–12cm) in diameter, is a breakfast favorite. Both of these can be baked in the oven.

The Rajasthani baati (*see pp132–133*) and the litti (*see pp138–139*) from Bihar, were not traditionally cooked in a tandoor, but within a cow-dung cake fire instead. The method given in this book details how to bake them in the oven at home.

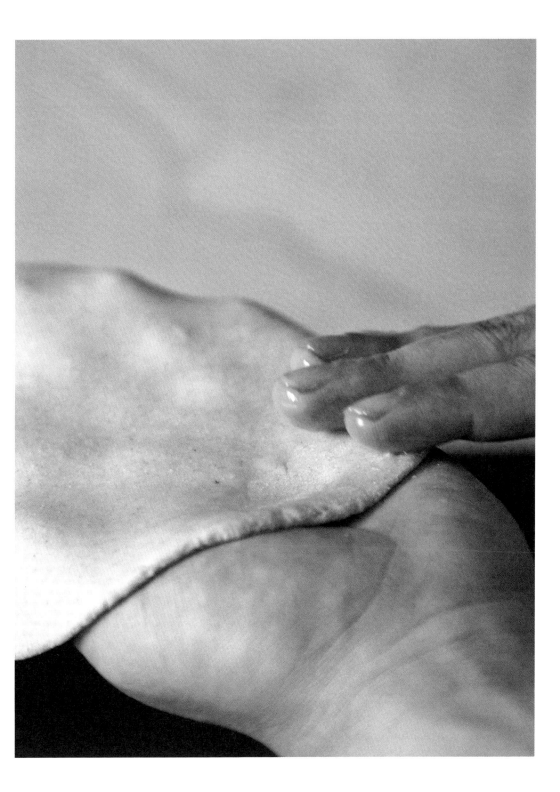

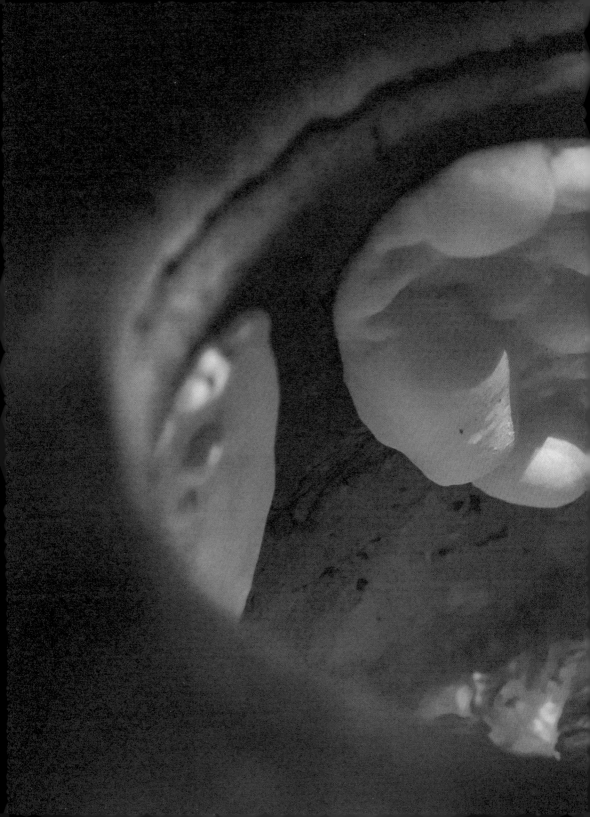

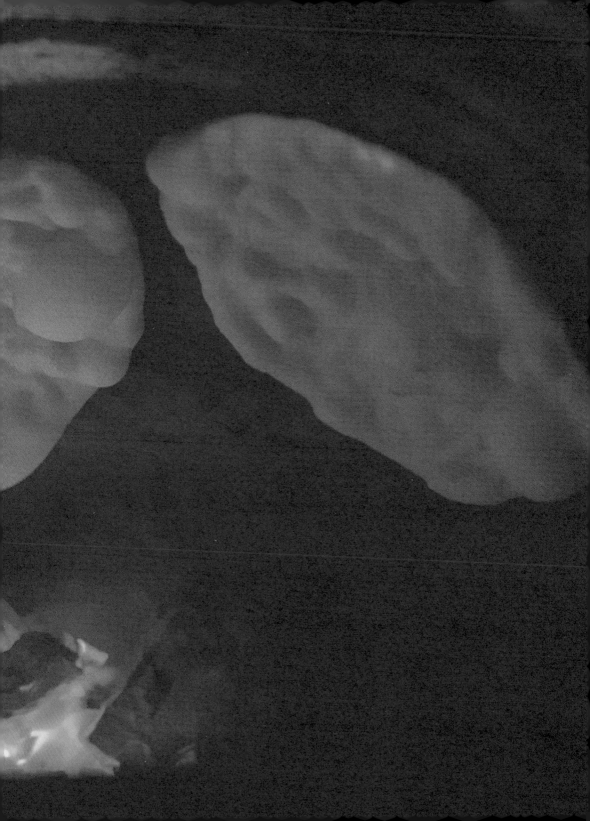

Tandoori roti

The difference in the taste and texture of a baked roti is quite surprising

Makes 6
Prep 45 minutes
Cook 15–20 minutes

9¾oz (280g) atta (whole wheat flour)
1 tsp salt
¼fl oz (10ml) vegetable oil

Set aside 1¼oz (35g) atta on a plate and place the remaining atta, salt, and oil in a deep bowl. Slowly add about 3½fl oz (105ml) of water, while kneading a pliable dough that does not stick to your hands or to the bowl. Cover and let rest for 30 minutes.

Preheat the oven, then divide the dough into 6 equal portions. Cover them again, so that the dough does not dry out while you are rolling the roti. Take 1 portion and shape it into a smooth ball between your palms. Flatten it under your fingers, turn it over in the plate of atta, and roll it out to about 6in (15cm) in diameter.

Brush off all the dry atta, wet your palms with water, and moisten both sides of the roti. Place the roti on the baking pan and bake for 5–6 minutes at 350°F (180°C), until brown spots appear on one side. Remove and serve hot.

If your oven is large enough, roll 3–4, moisten lightly, and place them on the pan in one go.

Perfect when crisp outside and chewy inside.

Kulcha, with matra

A popular street food in northern India

Makes 6
Prep 15 minutes
Rest 4 hours
Cook 15–20 minutes

9¾oz (280g) maida (all-purpose flour)
1 tsp salt
1 tsp baking powder
1fl oz (30ml) melted butter
1oz (30g) yogurt
½fl oz (15ml) ghee or ½oz (15g)
   butter to serve

For garnish
2oz (60g) fresh cilantro, minced
1½oz (45g) ginger, slivered
¼oz (10g) cumin seeds, roasted
   and ground
¼oz (10g) raw mango powder
1 tsp salt

Having set aside 1¼oz (35g) maida on a plate, place the remaining maida in a deep bowl. Mix in salt and baking powder, then crumble in the melted butter. Add the yogurt, and slowly adding 3½fl oz (105ml) water, knead until the dough is smooth and somewhat spongy. Cover with thin, damp cheesecloth and set aside for 4 hours.

Knead the risen dough again for a few minutes, then divide into 6 equal portions. Keep the dough covered with thin cheesecloth while rolling the kulchas, so that it does not dry out.

Mix all the ingredients for the garnish and set aside. Place a tava on medium heat to warm. Take 1 portion of dough and shape it into a smooth ball between your palms. Flatten it, turn it over in the platter of maida, and roll it out evenly to about 6in (15cm) in diameter. Sprinkle a little garnish on top of the kulcha and press it lightly into the dough with the rolling pin. Brush the other side of the kulcha with a little water and place it, moist-side down, on the warm tava. Cover and cook on low heat for a couple of minutes. Sprinkle with a little water and turn it over. The kulchas are perfect when light and fluffy.

Brush the kulchas with ½ tsp ghee or butter for added flavor.

FOR MATRA

3½ oz (105g) matra (dried white peas), soaked overnight

1 tsp salt

¼ tsp turmeric powder

½fl oz (15ml) vegetable oil

1–2 bay leaves

½oz (15g) ginger-garlic paste

3½oz (100g) onions, sliced

1 tsp garam masala

1 tsp cumin seeds, roasted and ground

1 tsp raw mango powder

½oz (15g) coriander powder

For garnish

1¾oz (50g) tomatoes, finely chopped

1oz (30g) fresh cilantro, chopped

2 green chiles, slit lengthwise (optional)

½oz (15g) ginger, julienned

1fl oz (30ml) lemon juice

Drain the matra and place in a pressure cooker with salt, a pinch of turmeric powder, and 9½fl oz (280ml) of water. Close the lid and bring to full pressure on medium heat, then allow to cook for another 10 minutes. Leave to cool.

Heat the vegetable oil in a heavy-based pan on medium heat. Add the bay leaves, then 30 seconds later, the ginger-garlic paste and onions. Cover and cook. When the onions are well glazed, add all the dry spices and cook for 1–2 minutes. Add the matra with any water remaining in the cooker—if none remains, add 2¼fl oz (70ml)—and mix well. Cover and leave to simmer for 10–15 minutes.

Garnish and serve hot with kulchas.

Variation To make pyaaz kulcha, mince 7½oz (210g) onions, 1oz (30g) fresh cilantro, and 2 green chiles (optional). Mix in 1 tsp raw mango powder, ¼oz (10g) roasted and ground cumin seeds, and 1oz (30g) salt. Set aside for 10 minutes, then squeeze out the water and divide into 6 portions. Knead the dough as for the plain kulcha and divide into 6 portions. Take 1 portion, roll it out to about 4in (10cm), and place the onion mix in the center, lift the edges to make a pouch, fill it with the mix, and seal. Roll it out again to 6in (15cm) and bake like a plain kulcha.

Lavasa

A versatile crisp flatbread from the Kashmir region

Makes 6
Prep 40 minutes
Rest 2 hours
Cook 1 hour

About ½ packet (4.5g) dry yeast
12¼oz (350g) maida
   (all-purpose flour)
1 tsp salt
1 tsp sugar
½fl oz (15ml) ghee

Warm 3½fl oz (105ml) water, add the dry yeast, mix well, and set aside to develop for about 30 minutes.

Set aside 1¼oz (35g) maida on a plate and mix the remaining maida, salt, and sugar in a deep bowl. Slowly add the yeast water, while kneading the maida into a pliable dough that does not stick to your hands or to the bowl. Coat the dough with ghee and set it aside for 2 hours.

Preheat the oven. Knead the dough again until the ghee is absorbed, then divide into 6 equal portions. Take 1 portion of dough and shape it into a smooth ball between your palms. Flatten it, turn it over in the plate of maida, and roll it out evenly to about 9in (23cm) in diameter. Place it on a greased baking pan and bake at 350°F (180°C), until the lavasa begins to brown—if your pan is large enough, you can bake more than one lavasa at a time. Serve hot.

Perfect when crisp yet soft.

Naan

The traditional accompaniment to North Indian curries

Makes 6

Prep 15 minutes

Rest 6 hours

Cook 40–60 minutes

9¾oz (280g) maida (all-purpose flour)

1 tsp salt

1 tsp baking powder

¼ tsp yeast

1 egg

2¼oz (70g) yogurt (if not using the
  egg, use an additional 1oz/30g)

½fl oz (15ml) vegetable oil

1fl oz (30ml) ghee

Having set aside 1¼oz (35g) maida on a plate, mix the remaining maida in a deep bowl with salt, baking powder, and yeast. Beat the egg and yogurt separately, then add these and the oil to the maida, and mix well. Slowly add about 1¼fl oz (35ml) water, while kneading the maida into a pliable dough that does not stick to your hands or to the bowl. Cover and let rest for 6 hours for the dough to rise.

Preheat the oven. Knead the risen dough again for a few minutes, then divide into 6 equal portions. Cover them with thin cheesecloth while rolling the naans, so the dough does not dry out. Take 1 portion of dough and shape it into a smooth ball between your palms. Flatten the ball, turn it over in the plate of maida, and roll it out evenly to about 7in (about 18cm) in diameter. The typical naan shape can be achieved by pulling out one side.

Lightly moisten one side of the naan and place this side down on a lightly greased baking pan. If they fit, roll out 3–4 naans, moisten one side, and place them on the tray together. Brush the tops lightly with 1 tsp ghee and bake in the oven at 400°F (200°C), until golden-brown spots begin to appear. Take out of the oven and serve hot.

Perfect when light and chewy.

PAIR IT WITH

SIRKA WALE PYAAZ

Place 9¾oz (280g) of peeled, washed, and dried pickling onions, 7½fl oz (210ml) white vinegar, 2oz (60g) sugar, and ¼oz (10g) salt in a clean, dry airtight bottle. Shake well and set aside for 2 days. Shake a couple of times in between.

Pudina naan

Imbued with the tangy flavors of fresh mint and raw mango

Makes 6

Prep 15 minutes

Rest 6 hours

Cook 40–60 min

9¾oz (280g) maida (all-purpose flour)

1 tsp salt

1 tsp baking powder

¾ tsp yeast

1 egg

2¼oz (70g) yogurt (if not using the egg, use an additional 1oz/30g)

½fl oz (15ml) vegetable oil

1¼fl oz (35ml) ghee

For flavoring

1oz (30g) white sesame seeds, roasted

1 tsp raw mango powder

½oz (15g) ginger, finely grated

1oz (30g) fresh cilantro, minced

1oz (30g) fresh mint, minced

2 green chiles (optional)

Grind together all the ingredients for flavoring and set aside.

Set aside 1¼oz (35g) of maida on a plate. Place the remaining maida in a deep bowl, mix in the salt, baking powder, and yeast, then add the flavoring, and mix. Beat the egg and yogurt separately, add these and the oil to the maida, and mix thoroughly. Slowly add about 1¼fl oz (35ml) water, while kneading the maida into a pliable dough that does not stick to your hands or to the bowl. Cover with thin cheesecloth and let rest for 6 hours for the dough to rise.

Preheat the oven. Knead the risen dough again for a few minutes, then divide it into 6 equal portions, and keep them covered so the dough does not dry out. Take 1 portion of dough and roll it into a smooth ball between your palms. Flatten the ball, turn it over in the plate of maida, and using a rolling pin, roll it out evenly to about 7in (about 18cm) in diameter. Pull one side to give it the typical naan shape and bake it the same way as you would a plain naan (*see p126*).

Perfect when the pudina and raw mango can be tasted.

Lehsuni naan

Brimming with mouthwatering aromas and garlic flavors

Makes 6
Prep 15 minutes
Rest 6 hours
Cook 40–60 min

9¾oz (280g) maida (all-purpose flour)

1½ tsp salt

1 tsp baking powder

¾ tsp yeast

¼oz (10g) red chili powder

1oz (30g) garlic paste

2oz (60g) onion paste

1 egg

2¼oz (70g) yogurt (if not using the
   egg, use an additional 1oz/30g)

1fl oz (30ml) vegetable oil

1¼fl oz (35ml) ghee

Having set aside 1¼oz (35g) maida on a plate, place the remaining maida in a deep bowl and add salt, baking powder, yeast, and red chili powder. Add the garlic paste and the onion paste, and mix well. Beat the egg and yogurt separately, then add these and the oil to the maida, and mix well again. Slowly add about 1¼fl oz (35ml) water, while kneading the maida into a pliable dough that does not stick to your hands or to the bowl. Cover with thin cheesecloth and let rest for 6 hours for the dough to rise.

Preheat the oven. Knead the risen dough again for a few minutes, then divide into 6 equal portions. Remember to keep these covered while rolling the naans, so the dough does not dry out. Take 1 portion of dough and roll it into a smooth ball between your palms. Flatten the ball, turn it over in the plate of maida, and using a rolling pin, roll it out evenly to about 7in (18cm) in diameter. Pull one side to a point to give it the typical naan shape and bake the same way as you would a plain naan *(see p126)*.

Perfect when crisp, yet light and chewy.

Paneer naan

A stand-alone bread enveloping a savory blend of spiced paneer

Makes 6
Prep 45 minutes
Rest 6 hours
Cook 1 hour

12¼oz (350g) maida (all-purpose flour)
1 tsp salt
1 tsp baking powder
¾ tsp yeast
1 egg
2¼oz (70g) yogurt (if not using the egg, use an additional 1oz/30g)
1fl oz (30ml) vegetable oil
1¼fl oz (35ml) ghee

For stuffing

210g (7½oz) paneer, not set
100g (3½oz) onions, minced
45g (1½oz) fresh coriander, minced
3–4 green chillies, minced (optional)
10g (¼oz) curry powder
1 tsp salt

Knead the dough as for a plain naan. The primary difference is in the quantity of maida, yeast, and vegetable oil, as each naan needs to be thicker to accommodate the filling—so the 6 portions of dough will be bigger.

Place the paneer and all the ingredients for the stuffing in a bowl and hand-mix to a smooth consistency. The mix will be granular but soft. Divide into 6 equal portions and set aside.

Preheat the oven. Take 1 portion of dough and shape into a smooth ball between your palms. Flatten the ball under your fingers, turn it over in the plate of maida, and roll out evenly to about 4in (10cm) in diameter. Place 1 portion of the paneer mix in the center, lift the edges to make a pouch, enclose the mix, and seal the dough pouch. Gently flatten the pouch, turn it over in the plate of maida, and roll it out to about 7in (18cm) in diameter. Pull one side to a point to give it the typical naan shape and bake as you would a plain naan (*see p126*).

Perfect when crisp outside, with a soft, creamy filling.

Keema naan

A meat version of the stuffed naan, ideal for a leisurely meal or a quick snack on the go

Makes 6
Prep 45 minutes
Rest 6 hours
Cook 1 hour

12¼oz (350g) maida (all-purpose flour)
1 tsp salt
1 tsp baking powder
¾ tsp yeast
1 egg
2¼oz (70g) yogurt (if not using the egg, use an additional 1oz/30g)
1fl oz (30ml) vegetable oil
1¼fl oz (35ml) ghee

For stuffing

1oz (30g) fresh cilantro, minced
7½oz (210g) chicken, minced
3½oz (100g) onion, minced
½oz (15g) ginger-garlic paste
½oz (15g) garam masala
½oz (15g) coriander powder
¼oz (10g) red chili powder
¼ tsp turmeric powder
1 tsp cumin powder
1 tsp salt

Prepare this in the same way as paneer naan *(see p130)*: the dough is made as for plain naan – the primary difference being the quantity of maida, yeast, and vegetable oil. The filling needs careful preparation.

Setting aside the fresh cilantro, place all the other stuffing ingredients in a pressure cooker and stir well. Add 4¾fl oz (140ml) water, close the lid and bring to full pressure on medium heat, then leave to cook for another 15 minutes. Allow to cool a little, then take off the lid, and cook on low heat until the water evaporates, almost to the point that the mince begins to stick to the bottom of the pressure-cooker pan. Transfer to a bowl, add the fresh cilantro, and mix well to a smooth consistency. Divide into 6 equal portions and set aside to cool.

Preheat the oven. Take 1 portion of dough and shape it into a smooth ball between your palms. Flatten it, turn it over in the plate of maida, and roll it out evenly to about (4in) 10cm in diameter. Place 1 portion of the keema mix in the center and carefully lift the edges of the dough to make a pouch, enclose the mix, and firmly seal the edges. Gently flatten the pouch, turn it over in the plate of maida, and roll it out to about 7in (about 18cm) in diameter. Pull one side out to get the typical naan shape and proceed to bake as you would a plain naan *(see p126)*.

Perfect when the keema is moist and flavorful.

Baati, with dal and churma

A traditional specialty from the state of Rajasthan

Makes 6

Prep 30 minutes

Cook 10–15 minutes

12¼oz (350g) atta (whole wheat flour)

1½ tsp salt

1 tsp baking powder

2¼fl oz (70ml) ghee

FOR DAL

1½oz (45g) split chickpeas

1½oz (45g) red lentils

1½oz (45g) pigeon peas

1½oz (45g) split green gram

1½oz (45g) split black gram

1½ tsp salt

¼ tsp turmeric powder

1fl oz (30ml) ghee

For tempering

1fl oz (30ml) ghee

¼oz (10g) cumin seeds

2–3 whole red chiles

1 tsp asafoetida powder

Mix the atta, salt, and baking powder in a deep bowl before crumbling in ½fl oz (15ml) ghee. Add about 4¾fl oz (140ml) water, while kneading the atta into a pliable, nonsticky dough. Cover and let rest for 30 minutes.

Preheat the oven. Divide the dough into 6 equal portions and keep them covered—a thin cheesecloth works well—while forming the baatis, so the dough does not dry out. Take 1 portion and shape it into a smooth ball between your palms. Flatten it under your fingers and gather it up again to form a hollow ball. Make sure you close the top well and again roll it into a smooth ball between your palms. Repeat with the remaining portions.

Place the baatis on a greased baking pan and bake at 400°F (200°C) for 10–15 minutes, turning them over and applying a little ghee once in between. The baatis should develop cracks on the surface. Take the baatis out of the oven.

To make the dal, mix all the lentils, wash well until the water runs clear, then soak, and set aside for 1 hour.

Drain and place the lentils in a pressure cooker. Add salt, turmeric powder, ghee, and 7fl oz (210ml) of water. Close the lid and bring to full pressure on medium heat, then leave to cook for 7–8 minutes, and set aside to cool.

Heat the ghee for tempering the dal in a heavy-based pan on medium heat; add the cumin seeds. Wait until they splutter, then add whole red chiles and asafoetida powder. When the chiles darken, add the ginger-garlic paste.

1oz (30g) ginger-garlic paste

1¼oz (35g) onion, chopped

1¼oz (35g) tomato, chopped

1 tsp red chili powder

1 tsp salt

1oz (30g) fresh cilantro,
chopped, for garnish

Stir well and cook on medium heat for 30 seconds. Add the onion, sauté until well glazed but not brown, then add the tomatoes and red chili powder, and stir. Cook until you have a masala of even consistency, then mix in the lentils and leave to simmer for 2–3 minutes. Garnish with fresh cilantro.

Take the baatis, pour about ¼fl oz (10ml) ghee over each one, and serve with dal and churma.

Perfect when turns golden brown and splits open.

TO MAKE

CHURMA

Take 3-4 baatis and crumble them to a slightly granular texture. Transfer to a bowl, add 1½oz (45g) sugar and 2fl oz (60ml) hot ghee. Mix well and serve with dal and baati. Adjust the sugar to taste—churma should not be too sweet.

Tsot

A breakfast bread from the Kashmir region

Makes 6
Prep 40 minutes
Rest 4 hours
Cook 1 hour

½oz (15g) dry yeast
1¼ tsp sugar
12¼oz (350g) maida
   (all-purpose flour)
½ tsp salt
1 tsp baking powder
1fl oz (30ml) ghee
½oz (15g) yogurt
1fl oz (30ml) milk
1oz (30g) poppy seeds

Mix the dry yeast and sugar to 3½fl oz (105ml) of warm water, and set aside to develop for about 30 minutes.

Set aside 1¼oz (35g) maida on a plate. Place the remaining maida in a deep bowl, mix in salt and baking powder, then crumble in ghee and yogurt. Slowly add the yeast water, while kneading a pliable dough that does not stick to your hand or to the bowl. Knead the dough for 5 minutes so that it becomes very soft, then coat with ghee, cover, and let rest for 4 hours or until it has risen to double its size.

Preheat the oven. Knead the dough again, then divide into 6 equal portions. Remember to keep the dough covered with thin cheesecloth while rolling the tsot, so that it does not dry out. Take 1 portion and shape it into a smooth ball between your palms. Flatten the ball, turn it over in the platter of maida, and roll it out evenly to about 8in (20cm) in diameter (tsot is thicker than lavasa).

Use the blunt side of the knife, or your fingers, to make long parallel indentations, about 0.04in (1 mm) apart, across the center, leaving a ½-in (1-cm) border along the edges. Brush the tsot with milk and sprinkle poppy seeds on it.

Place on a preheated tava and cook on low heat for 3–4 minutes on one side only—do not turn it over. Remove and bake at 350°F (180°C) in the preheated oven for 2–3 minutes, until it turns a soft golden brown. Take out and serve hot.

Perfect when the crust is slightly crisp and the inside chewy.

Litti, with chokha

A stuffed, savory bread from the state of Bihar

Makes 6
Prep 1 hour
Cook 25–30 minutes

9¾oz (280g) atta (whole wheat flour)
5oz (140g) sooji (semolina flour)
1 tsp salt
1 tsp baking powder
½fl oz (15ml) ghee

For stuffing
5oz (140g) sattu atta
   (roasted gram flour)
3½oz (100g) onion, minced
1½oz (45g) fresh cilantro, minced
½oz (15g) ginger, minced
2–3 green chiles, minced (optional)
1 tsp cumin seeds, roasted and
   ground
½fl oz (15ml) ghee
1 tsp salt

Mix the two flours, salt, and baking powder in a deep bowl, then rub in the ghee. Slowly add about 4¾fl oz (140ml) of water, while kneading the flours into a pliable, nonsticky dough. Cover with thin cheesecloth and let rest for 30 minutes.

Preheat the oven. Place the sattu atta in a bowl, and one by one, add all the ingredients for the stuffing, while mixing. Adding the onion will moisten the mix so that it binds when held within a fist. Divide into 6 equal portions and set aside.

To make the littis, divide the dough into 6 equal portions. Make sure they do not dry out while you are rolling the litti by ensuring they remain covered. Take 1 dough ball and pinch it between your fingers and thumb into a small bowl shape. Fill the hollow with 1 portion of the stuffing and gather the mouth of the dough bowl to close it. Then shape the whole into a smooth ball between your palms. When all the littis have been made, place them on a greased baking pan and bake at 400°F (200°C) for 15–20 minutes. They are perfect when they are golden brown and crisp.

FOR CHOKHA

8¾oz (250g) eggplant

7oz (200g) tomatoes

½fl oz (15ml) mustard oil

½oz (15g) garlic, minced

3½oz (100g) potato, boiled

3½oz (100g) onion, minced

1oz (30g) green chiles, minced
  (optional)

1½oz (45g) fresh cilantro, minced

¼oz (10g) ginger, minced

1oz (30g) lemon juice

¼oz (10g) salt

To make the chokha, wash and dry the eggplant and tomatoes, and lightly rub all over with mustard oil. Score the eggplant in 2–3 places, press the minced garlic into the slits, then roast on a wire mesh placed over an open flame, turning over regularly so it roasts evenly from all sides (or grill until charred on each side). When the skin begins to split, it is done. Set aside. Roast the tomatoes and the boiled potatoes in the same manner.

Place the eggplant and tomatoes in a large bowl while still hot, pour 2¼fl oz (70 ml) of hot water over them, cover, and set aside for 5 minutes. Take them out of the water, cut off the stem of the eggplant, and then remove the eggplant and tomato skins. In a shallow dish, first mash the eggplant and tomatoes together, then mash in the potatoes—for an extra tang, you can add a dash of mustard oil, ½fl oz (15 ml), at this stage. Mix all the other ingredients and set aside.

Lightly crush each litti, pour ghee (to taste) over them, and serve hot with chokha.

Bakarkhani

A sweet bread popular in northern India

Makes 6

Prep 1 hour

Cook 1 hour

12¼oz (350g) maida (all-purpose flour)

1 tsp salt

¼oz (10g) sugar

1 tsp baking powder

1 tsp green cardamom powder

3½fl oz (105ml) ghee, of which 2fl oz (60ml) is for the dough

5½fl oz (165ml) milk

1½ tsp white poppy seeds

Set aside 1¼oz (35g) maida on a plate and mix the remaining maida, salt, sugar, baking powder, and green cardamom powder in a deep bowl. Crumble in the ghee. Slowly add 3½fl oz (105ml) warm milk, while kneading the maida into a pliable dough that does not stick to your hand or to the bowl. Knead the dough for an extra 5 minutes, then roll it into a large ball. Flatten it under your fingers, turn it over in the plate of maida, and roll it out evenly, as thinly as possible.

Spread about ½fl oz (15ml) ghee on the surface and sprinkle some dry maida over it. Fold over both sides, overlaying the edges, carefully spreading ¼fl oz (10ml) ghee over the whole area, and fold again. Next, spread 1 tsp ghee over the length and fold again twice, so that you have a layered square of dough. Cut this neatly into 6 equal portions.

Take 1 portion, shape it into a smooth ball between your palms, flatten it, and roll it into a slightly oval-shaped disk of about 4in (10cm). Do this with each portion, then place them on a greased baking pan. Firmly prick the surface of each bakarkhani with the tines of a fork but do not make a hole. Brush with ¼oz (10ml) milk and sprinkle with ½ tsp white poppy seeds. Bake in a preheated oven at 400°F (200°C) until the bakarkhani are golden brown. Serve hot.

Perfect when soft and flaky, with a crisp crust.

Sheermal

A rich, golden sweetbread brushed with saffron milk

Makes 6
Prep 40 minutes
Rest 2 hours
Cook 1 hour

¼ tsp saffron
2¼fl oz (70ml) milk
12¼oz (350g) maida
   (all-purpose flour)
½ tsp salt
2oz (60g) sugar
2¼fl oz (70ml) ghee

Soak the saffron in ½fl oz (15ml) milk and set aside.

Set aside 1¼oz (35g) maida on a plate, then in a deep bowl, mix salt and sugar in the remaining maida. Add the ghee and the remaining milk, while kneading the maida into a pliable dough that does not stick to your hand or to the bowl. Cover and set aside for 2 hours.

Preheat the oven. Knead the dough again, then divide into 6 equal portions. To keep the dough from drying as you roll out the sheermal, cover it with thin cheesecloth. Take 1 portion of dough and shape it into a smooth ball between your palms. Flatten it, turn it over in the plate of maida, and roll it out evenly to about 7in (17cm) in diameter. Sheermal is a chunky bread, and it may seem a little thick when rolling it out. Indent the surface with the tines of a fork at regular intervals.

Place on a greased baking pan and bake at 400°F (200°C), turning it over once or twice in between, until the sheermal becomes a nice golden brown in color. Brush with the saffron milk and serve hot.

Perfect when soft, flaky, and aromatic.

FRY IN
THE KADHAI

◆◆◆◆◆◆◆◆◆◆◆◆◆◆◆◆◆◆◆◆◆◆◆◆◆◆

Introduction

Puri, the most well-known, deep-fried Indian bread, is not an everyday bread in most homes—it is much more likely to be a weekend brunch treat, and is a definitive festival and celebration special across the length and breadth of the country.

The dough preparation for puris is much the same as for rotis and parathas. The main difference being that puris can also be made with a mix of whole wheat and refined flour, or just refined flour. In addition, the dough can be used as soon as it is kneaded and does not necessarily have to be set aside to enhance its elasticity.

As with other breads, a wide choice of ingredients may be added to the dough. Having said that, however, there are very few varieties of stuffed puris. The popular breakfast bedmi (*see p172*) was traditionally a stuffed puri, but today, the ingredients are more often mixed into the flour before kneading—it is also possible to buy premixed, packaged bedmi flour. While there is no doubt that it simplifies the making of a bedmi, it certainly does take away from the authentic flavor.

Once the dough is ready, place the oil to heat in a kadhai while rolling out the puris. There is no standard size for puris—they can be made large or small according to preference. When rolling them out, it is best not to use any dry flour as it can flake off and burn in the oil, potentially giving the puris a burned appearance as well as taste.

As an alternative, use a drop of oil to prevent the dough from sticking to the work surface while rolling. If rolling puris proves challenging, a small amount of dry flour can be used, but be sure to dust off as much as possible before frying the puri. It is perfectly fine to roll out several puris in advance and set them aside. Once the oil reaches the appropriate temperature, they can be fried quickly in succession, making it easier to prepare a large batch for serving. This efficiency is likely why puris have been, and continue to be, a popular choice for large gatherings.

The kadhai, a deep, inverted, dome-shaped vessel with a broad base that sweeps up to a wide-open mouth, is critical to the process of

deep frying. The shape perfectly complements the function for which it is designed. The concave base, in direct contact with the heat, is where the oil gathers. The deep core, therefore, is where the oil is hottest. This is important because a puri will puff up into the characteristic ball-like shape only when it is entirely submerged in hot oil.

This also means that the greatest care must be taken to slip the puris into the oil gently, and at an angle from the edge of the kadhai, to prevent the hot oil from splattering. When slipped in at an angle, the puri will sink to the bottom and drown in the hot oil, cooking quickly before rising slowly to the relatively less-hot surface. The wide curvature of the kadhai allows free movement of the long-handled jhara used to flip the puri, brown it to satisfaction, and remove from the hot oil.

Puris remain soft and edible for a longer period as compared to rotis or parathas. To store puris, allow them to cool completely and then place them in an insulated container.

The puri is a weekend brunch treat, a definitive festival and celebration special across the length and breadth of the country, and a popular choice for large gatherings.

They can be kept in the refrigerator for up to two days, but should be brought to room temperature before being served. Puris cannot be refried, or heated in an oven or a microwave, as this will cause them to release oil and become unappetizing.

For Indian festivals that require grain-free fasting, puris made from plant-based flours offer a nutritious alternative. Popular options include puris made from kuttu (buckwheat) flour (*see pp168–169*) and singhara (water chestnut) flour (*see pp168–169*). As these flours are generally gluten-free, a binding agent such as potato is usually used to knead the dough.

Bhatura (*see pp176–179*) is another popular deep-fried bread, which is especially well-loved in northern India and gradually gaining popularity across the country. Although they are not particularly difficult to make, bhaturas are not commonly prepared at home. Instead, almost every Indian fast-food outlet

serves them with the traditional pairing of chhole. Recent experimentation and innovation have led to exciting versions, including stuffed bhaturas and those with added ingredients in the dough.

Bhaturas are made from refined flour. After kneading the dough, it must be set aside to ferment. Generally, the dough should be left to rise for 3–4 hours if the ambient temperature is around 85°F (30°C) or higher, and for 6 hours if it is cooler. Once the dough has fermented, kneading it a little more will make it more pliable and easier to roll out. Unlike puris, bhaturas must be fried individually as they are rolled out. They cannot be rolled and set aside to fry later because the dough will shrink if kept. Always heat the oil to the correct temperature before starting to roll out the bhaturas.

Another unique feature that defines bhaturas and make them a popular fixture at commercial establishments is that they can be

fried once and kept aside. At this stage, they are left slightly underdone, so that as and when required, they can be refried without turning too brown or looking overdone, and then be served hot and fresh. This is important, as bhaturas have to be eaten freshly fried for maximum enjoyment. They cannot be stored or refried a third time. Of course, at home they can be cooked to perfection in the first frying.

Bhaturas and puris aren't the only deep-fried breads made in India. There are a wide variety of specialties from different regions. The Bengali luchi (*see pp162–165*) is well known, while Madhya Pradesh offers the distinctive Indori palak puri (*see pp170–171*). There is also the babru (*see pp180–181*), from the mountains of Himachal Pradesh, which is rapidly making its way into the heart of India.

Puri, with gholia aloo

Deep-fried bread and a spicy potato curry, perfect for festivals and celebrations

Makes 6

Prep 40 minutes

Cook 12–15 minutes

9¾oz (280g) atta (whole wheat flour)

9½fl oz (280ml) vegetable oil,
    for frying

FOR GHOLIA ALOO

½fl oz (15ml) vegetable oil

1 tsp cumin seeds

½ tsp asafoetida powder

¼ tsp turmeric powder

1 tsp cumin seeds, roasted
    and ground

1 tsp red chili powder

1 tsp salt

9¾oz (280g) potatoes, cut
    into 1-in (2½-cm) cubes

2¼oz (70g) yogurt

Use a deep bowl to knead the atta into a pliable nonsticky dough, with about 3½fl oz (105ml) water, added slowly. Cover with thin cheesecloth and let rest for 30 minutes.

Divide the dough into 6 equal portions. Keep them covered while rolling the puris, so the dough does not dry out. Take one portion and shape it into a smooth ball between your palms. Flatten it gently and roll it out evenly to about 6–7in (15–17cm) in diameter. If the dough sticks, smear a touch of oil over the work surface. Roll out all the puris.

Heat the oil in a heavy-based kadhai on medium heat—it should not start smoking. If a pinch of dough dropped in the oil floats to the top, it is hot enough. Gently ease the puri into the oil from the edge of the kadhai. When it rises, use a perforated, long-handled spatula to flip it over and cook the other side until golden brown—this will take only a few seconds. Then remove and drain. The puris are well done when they are puffed up, with one side soft and the other crisp.

To make gholia aloo, heat the oil in a heavy-based pan on medium heat. Add the cumin seeds, and when they start to splutter, add all the dry spices and salt. Stir, then add the potatoes and stir again. Add 12fl oz (350ml) of

For garnish

1oz (30g) fresh cilantro, chopped

½oz (15g) ginger, julienned

2 green chiles, chopped (optional)

water, and leave to simmer until the potatoes are soft and the water has reduced to half.

Beat the yogurt to a smooth consistency. Smash the potatoes a little, turn off the heat, pour in the yogurt, and mix well. Garnish with fresh cilantro, ginger, and green chiles (if using), and serve hot with puris.

Luchi, with panch phoran aloo

A Bengali take on puri and an aromatic, spiced potato medley

Makes 6
Prep 45 minutes
Cook 12–15 minutes

9¾oz (280g) maida (all-purpose flour)
1 tsp salt
¼ tsp sugar
1½fl oz (45ml) ghee
9½fl oz (280ml) vegetable oil,
   for frying

FOR PANCH PHORAN ALOO
½fl oz (15ml) mustard oil
¼oz (10g) panch phoran*
2 whole red chiles
¼ tsp turmeric powder
1 tsp asafoetida powder
1 tsp salt

Place the maida, salt, and sugar in a deep bowl and crumble in the ghee. Warm 3½fl oz (105ml) of water and add slowly, while kneading the flour into a pliable dough that does not stick to your hand or to the bowl. Cover with thin cheesecloth and let rest for 30 minutes. Knead the dough again—it should be stiff enough to roll without turning it in the flour—and divide into 6 equal portions. Cover the dough to prevent it drying while rolling the luchi. Take one portion and shape it into a smooth ball between your palms. Flatten it, and roll it out evenly to about 15cm (6in) in diameter. Roll out all the luchis.

Heat the oil in a heavy-based kadhai on medium heat. Test the oil by dropping in a pinch of dough—if it floats to the top, the oil is hot enough. Gently ease one luchi into the oil from the edge of the kadhai. When it rises, use a perforated, long-handled spatula to flip it over and cook the other side until golden brown. Remove and drain. The luchis are well done when they are incredibly soft.

To make the aloo, heat the mustard oil in a heavy-based pan on medium heat but do not let it reach smoking point,

7½oz (210g) potatoes, cut
into 1-in (2½-cm) cubes
1 tsp sugar (optional)

*a combination, in equal proportion,
of black mustard, nigella, fenugreek,
fennel, and cumin seeds

and add the panch phoran. When the panch phoran starts to splutter, add the red chiles, followed by the remaining dry spices and salt. Add the potatoes and stir well. Add 9½fl oz (280ml) of water and cook on low heat for about 15 minutes, until the potatoes are soft and the curry thickens. Add the sugar (if using) and adjust the salt if necessary. Serve hot with luchis.

Methi ki puri

Puri infused with fresh fenugreek leaves for additional zest

Makes 6
Prep 1 hour
Cook 12–15 minutes

9¾oz (280g) atta (whole wheat flour)
5oz (140g) fenugreek leaves, minced
¼ oz (10g) red chili powder
¼ oz (10g) cumin seeds, roasted
   and ground
1 tsp salt
9½fl oz (280ml) vegetable oil,
   for frying

Place the atta, fenugreek leaves, and the rest of the ingredients—except for the oil—in a deep bowl and mix well. Slowly add 3½fl oz (105ml) water, while kneading the atta into a pliable dough that does not stick to your hand or to the bowl. Cover with thin cheesecloth and let rest for 30 minutes.

Divide the dough into 6 equal portions. Cover them again while rolling the puris, so the dough does not dry out. Take one portion and shape it into a smooth ball between your palms. Flatten the ball and roll it out evenly to about 6in (15cm) in diameter. Repeat until all the puris are rolled out.

Heat the oil in a heavy-based kadhai on medium heat—it should not be so hot that it starts smoking. Test the oil by dropping in a pinch of dough—if it floats to the top, the oil is hot enough. Gently ease the puri into the oil from the edge of the kadhai. When it rises, use a perforated, long-handled spatula to flip it over and cook the other side until golden brown. Remove, drain, and serve hot.

Perfect when soft, chewy, and aromatic.

PAIR IT WITH
BOONDI RAITA

Add 1 tsp salt to 6¼oz (175g) yogurt, and whisk well. Mix in 1¼oz (35g) minced cilantro and 2 minced green chiles (optional). Add 3½oz (105g) of boondi just before serving, or else it will become soggy. Serve cold.

Singhare ke atte ki puri

Gluten-free puri made from water-chestnut flour, traditionally prepared during fasting

Makes 6

Prep 20 minutes

Cook 12–15 minutes

9¾oz (280g) singhara atta
(water-chestnut flour)

1 tsp raw mango powder

1 tsp salt

3½oz (100g) potatoes, boiled
and peeled

1oz (30g) fresh cilantro, minced

9½fl oz (280ml) vegetable oil,
for frying

Place the singhara atta in a deep bowl; add in the raw mango powder and salt, and mix. Mash the potatoes, rub into the singhara atta, then add the fresh cilantro and mix well. Knead and make a pliable dough, so that it does not stick to your hand or to the bowl. The potato will act as a binder—do not add water unless absolutely necessary. Divide the dough into 6 equal portions. Cover them with thin cheesecloth while rolling the puris, so the dough doesn't dry out.

Apply a little oil to your palms and shape 1 portion of dough into a smooth ball. Flatten it with your fingers, then pat it from palm to palm to extend it as much as possible. This dough will stick while rolling it out, so spread a plastic sheet on the work surface and roll out the dough on it to about 5in (13cm) in diameter. Carefully lift the plastic sheet, place with the rolled-out roti face down on a tray, and peel away the plastic. Repeat until all the puris are rolled out.

Heat the oil in a heavy-based kadhai on medium heat. Test the oil by dropping in a pinch of dough—if it floats to the top, the oil is hot enough. Ease the puri into the oil from the edge of the kadhai. When it rises, use a perforated, long-handled spatula to flip it over and cook the other side until golden brown. Remove, drain, and serve hot.

Perfect when soft and crumbly.

Variation To make kuttu ke atte ki puri, take 9¾oz (280g) kuttu atta (buckwheat flour), add 3½oz (100g) boiled potatoes, ¼ tsp turmeric powder, ¼oz (10g) roasted and ground cumin seeds, 1½ tsp salt, 1oz (30g) minced fresh cilantro, and 2–3 green chiles (optional). Knead into dough with 4fl oz (120ml) warm water, roll out, and fry the puris, as you would for singhare ke atte ki puri.

Indori puri palak ki

Spinach-flavored puri from the city of Indore in central India

Makes 6

Prep 25 minutes

Cook 15–20 minutes

14¼oz (420g) spinach, chopped

1oz (30g) yogurt

¼oz (10g) ginger, minced

¼ tsp turmeric powder

¼ oz (10g) cumin seeds

2 green chiles

1oz (30g) fresh cilantro, chopped

9¾ oz (280g) atta (whole wheat flour)

1 tsp salt

10fl oz (300ml) vegetable oil,
    for frying

PAIR IT WITH

MOOLI LACCHA

Peel and grate 7½oz (210g) daikon in a large bowl. Add 1 tsp roasted and ground cumin seeds, ½ tsp red chili powder, 1 minced green chile (optional), ½oz (15g) minced fresh cilantro, 1oz (30g) fresh mint, 1 tsp of salt, and toss well. Add 1fl oz (30ml) lemon juice, toss again, and serve fresh.

Having washed, drained, and blanched the spinach, blend it in a food processor together with yogurt, ginger, turmeric powder, cumin seeds, green chiles, and fresh cilantro—do not add water. Place the atta in a deep bowl, add the salt and ½fl oz (15ml) oil, and mix well. Knead the spinach into the atta to make it into a pliable, nonsticky dough. Add water only if necessary. Divide the dough into 6 equal portions and cover them with thin cheesecloth, so the dough does not dry out while rolling out the puris.

Apply a little oil to your palms, take 1 portion, and shape it into a smooth ball. Flatten it, pat it from palm to palm to extend it as much as possible, then roll it out with a rolling pin to about 6in (15cm) in diameter. Repeat until all the puris are rolled out.

Heat the oil in a heavy-based kadhai on medium heat—make sure it does not get so hot that it starts smoking. Test the oil by dropping in a pinch of dough—if it floats to the top, the oil is hot enough. Gently ease the puri into the oil from the edge of the kadhai. When it rises, use a perforated, long-handled spatula to flip it over and cook the other side until golden brown. Remove, drain, and serve hot.

Perfect when soft on one side, crisp on the other.

Bedmi, with kaddu

Spiced lentil puri and pumpkin curry, a favorite from Chandni Chowk in Old Delhi

Makes 6
Prep 1 hour
Cook 12–15 minutes

9¾oz (280g) atta (whole wheat flour)
2¼oz (70g) maida (all-purpose flour)
10¼fl oz (310ml) vegetable oil
¼ tsp turmeric powder
¼oz (10g) red chili powder
1 tsp asafoetida powder
1 tsp raw mango powder
¼oz (10g) cumin seeds, roasted
   and ground
1½ tsp salt
3½oz (105g) skinned black lentil,
   coarsely ground

FOR KADDU
1fl oz (30ml) vegetable oil
½ tsp fenugreek seeds
1 tsp fennel seeds
1–2 whole red chiles
¼ tsp turmeric powder

Set aside 1¼oz (35g) of atta on a plate and place the remaining flour in a deep bowl. Slowly add about 3½fl oz (105ml) of water, while kneading the flour into a pliable, nonsticky dough. Cover and let rest for 30 minutes.

Heat 1fl oz (30ml) of oil in a heavy-based pan, add all the dry masalas and salt, stir well, add the skinned black lentils, and stir thoroughly until well mixed. Add 2¼fl oz (70ml) water, and cook until the water is fully absorbed and the mix is dry. Allow it to cool. Then divide the mix into 6 equal portions.

Divide the dough into 6 equal portions. Cover them with thin cheesecloth while rolling the bedmi, so that the dough does not dry out. Take 1 portion and shape it into a smooth ball between your palms. Flatten it and roll it out evenly to about 5in (13cm) in diameter. Place a portion of the lentil mix in the center, lift the edges to make a pouch that encloses the mix, and close the mouth. Gently flatten the pouch and roll it out again to about 5in (13cm) in diameter. Repeat until all the bedmis are rolled out. Cover them with the cheesecloth so they do not dry out.

Heat the remaining oil on medium heat in a heavy-based kadhai. Test the oil by dropping in a pinch of dough—if it

1 tsp salt

1lb 2oz (500g) pumpkin, cut into 1-in (2½-cm) cubes

¼oz (10g) raw mango powder

1oz (30g) sugar

½oz (15g) fresh cilantro, chopped, for garnish

floats to the top, the oil is hot enough. Gently ease the bedmis into the oil from the edge of the kadhai. When it rises, use a perforated, long-handled spatula to flip it over and cook the other side until golden brown. Remove and drain. The bedmis are well done when they are crispy.

To make the kaddu, heat the oil on medium heat in a heavy-based pan. Reduce the heat and add the fenugreek seeds, fennel seeds, whole red chiles, turmeric powder, and salt. Stir for a few seconds and add the pumpkin. Stir well, cover, and cook for 7–10 minutes, stirring once or twice in between. Add 4¾fl oz (140ml) of water, and cook on medium heat for 15 minutes until the pumpkin is soft. Add the raw mango powder and sugar, stir well, and cook for another 5 minutes, stirring as needed, until the kaddu has become a little mushy. Garnish with cilantro and serve hot with bedmis.

Bhatura, with chana

Fluffy, deep-fried bread and spiced chickpea curry, a beloved North Indian combination

Makes 8
Rest 5–6 hours
Prep 45 minutes
Cook 40 minutes

9¾oz (280g) maida (all-purpose flour)
5oz (140g) sooji (semolina flour)
1½ tsp salt
1 tsp baking powder
1oz (30g) yogurt
10¼fl oz (310ml) vegetable oil

FOR CHANA
5oz (140g) whole chickpeas,
    soaked overnight
1 tsp cumin seeds
1 tsp salt
1fl oz (30ml) vegetable oil
3½oz (100g) onion, finely chopped
½oz (15g) ginger-garlic paste

Set aside 1¼oz (35g) of maida on a plate and place the remaining maida and all of the sooji in a deep bowl. Add salt and baking powder, and dry mix the ingredients. Add the yogurt and 1fl oz (30ml) oil to get a crumbly consistency, then slowly add 3½fl oz (105ml) of water, while kneading the flours to a pliable, nonsticky dough. Cover and set aside for 5–6 hours.

Place the remaining oil in a heavy-based kadhai on medium heat. Divide the dough into 8 equal portions. Keep them covered with thin cheesecloth while rolling out the bhatura, so that they do not dry out. Take 1 portion and roll it into a smooth ball between your palms. Flatten it and roll it out evenly to about 7in (17cm) in diameter.

Test how hot the oil is by dropping in a pinch of dough—if it floats to the top, the oil is hot enough. Gently ease the bhatura into the oil from the edge of the kadhai. When it rises, use a perforated, long-handled spatula to flip it over and cook the other side until golden brown. Remove and drain. The bhaturas are well done when they are nicely puffed up but not brown.

To make the chana, drain and place the whole chickpeas in a pressure cooker with the cumin seeds, salt, and 9½fl oz (280ml) of water. Close the lid, bring it to full

3½oz (100g) tomato, finely chopped

½ tsp turmeric powder

1½oz (45g) coriander powder

¼oz (10g) cumin seeds, roasted
and ground

1oz (30g) chana masala

1–2 green chiles, chopped, for garnish

1oz (30g) fresh cilantro, chopped
for garnish

pressure on medium heat, and then cook for another 10 minutes. Take off heat and set aside to cool.

Heat the oil in a heavy-based pan on medium heat, add the onions and ginger-garlic paste, cover, cook for 5 minutes, and add the tomatoes. Cover and cook again until the mix is well done but not too brown. Add the dry spices and stir well. Add the pressure-cooked chickpeas as well as the liquid left in the cooker. Adjust the salt to taste. Reduce the heat and leave to simmer for 7–8 minutes. The chana should be thick and soupy rather than watery, so let any excess water evaporate.

Garnish with green chiles and fresh cilantro, and serve with bhaturas.

Variation To make a paneer bhatura, mix 7½oz (210g) paneer, 1oz (30g) minced fresh cilantro, 1 tsp each of red chili powder and roasted and ground cumin seeds, and 1½ tsp salt to a smooth consistency, and divide into 8 equal portions. Knead the dough and portion it as for plain bhaturas. Roll out each portion to about 5in (13cm) in diameter, lift the edges to make a pouch, fill it with one portion of the mix, and seal. Roll it out again to about 7in (18cm) and fry.

Babru

A sweet or savory breakfast bread from the state of Himachal Pradesh

Makes 6–8
Rest 1 hour
Prep 1 hour
Cook 20–25 minutes

7½oz (210g) jaggery
9¾oz (280g) atta (whole wheat flour)
¼ tsp salt
1 tsp baking powder
1oz (30g) yogurt
1 tsp fennel seeds, crushed
7fl oz (210ml) vegetable oil, for frying

Dissolve the jaggery in 3½fl oz (105ml) of warm water and set aside to cool. Place the atta in a deep bowl, add the salt and baking powder, and mix well. Add the yogurt and fennel seeds, and keep mixing. Slowly add the cooled jaggery water, while kneading the atta into a pliable dough that does not stick to your hand or to the bowl. Cover and set aside for 1 hour.

Knead the dough once more. Divide the dough into 6–8 equal portions. Cover them with thin cheesecloth while rolling the babru, so the dough does not dry out. Take 1 portion and shape it into a smooth ball between your palms. Flatten it, and roll it out evenly to about 4in (10cm) in diameter. Repeat until all the babrus are rolled out.

Heat the oil on medium heat in a heavy-based kadhai—test the oil by dropping in a pinch of dough—if it floats to the top, the oil is hot enough. Gently ease the babru into the oil from the edge of the kadhai. When it rises to the top, use a perforated, long-handled spatula to flip it over and cook until golden brown. Remove and drain. It's best to fry the babru individually, unless you have a large kadhai that will take 2–3 of them together. Serve hot.

Perfect when golden brown, but soft and chewy inside.

Roth

A sweet bread from the state of Kashmir, shared to celebrate joy and good fortune

Makes 6
Prep 45 minutes
Cook 15–20 minutes

9¾oz (280g) atta (whole wheat flour)
9¾oz (280g) maida (all-purpose flour)
1½oz (45g) sugar, powdered
1½oz (45g) green cardamom seeds,
    crushed
1fl oz (30ml) ghee
4¾fl oz (140ml) milk
2¼oz (70g) almonds, crushed
2¼oz (70g) raisins
1oz (30g) poppy seeds
9½fl oz (280ml) vegetable oil,
    for frying

Having set aside 1¼oz (35g) of atta on a plate, place the remaining atta and maida in a deep bowl, add the sugar and green cardamom seeds, and crumble in the ghee. Knead to a pliable, nonsticky dough while slowly adding the milk. Cover and set aside for 1 hour.

Divide the dough into 6 equal portions. Remember to cover them with thin cheesecloth while rolling the roth, so the dough does not dry out. Take 1 portion and shape it into a smooth ball between your palms. Flatten it and roll it out evenly to about 8in (20cm) in diameter and ¼in (½cm) in thickness. Press in 2 tbsp of almonds and raisins, and 1 tsp of poppy seeds onto each roth.

Heat the oil on medium heat in a heavy-based kadhai—not so hot that it starts smoking. Test the oil by dropping in a pinch of dough—if it floats to the top, the oil is hot enough. Gently ease the roth into the oil from the edge of the kadhai and fry until golden brown. Remove, drain, and serve hot.

Perfect when golden brown, with a cake-like texture.

Glossary

A

aam mango

achar pickle

adrak ginger

aloo potato

anda egg

B

bhari to be filled with

bind the dough kneading warms the strands of gluten present in flour, causing them to expand and stick together to form an elastic dough. When kneading gluten-free flour, a binding agent, such as potato, has to be added to form a pliable dough.

boondi small, round, crunchy, chickpea-flour fritters that can be plain, salted, or spiced.

C

chana chickpea

chapati one of the many names for the roti, phulka, rotli, and poli, among others. Generally, a chapati is bigger and thicker than a phulka.

chulah an earthen or brick stove that was usually coal or wood fired.

cow-dung cakes a mix of cow or buffalo dung, husk, and straw, patted into a thick disk and sun dried. Traditionally burned as fuel in India.

curry gravy

D

dal pulses or the edible seeds of legumes such as black gram, red lentils, chickpeas, and kidney beans.

dhania cilantro

do palli two layers

G

gajar carrot

gujiya a sweet, deep-fried dumpling traditionally made for Holi festivities.

garam masala a mix of aromatic spices, such as cumin seeds, green cardamom, cinnamon, cloves, black pepper, and nutmeg.

ghee clarified butter

gobi cauliflower

grain-free fasting ritual fast during which the consumption of any kind of grain is prohibited, but other foods may be consumed.

H

hari mirch green chile

J

jolada jowar or sorgum

K

kaddu pumpkin

kamrak star fruit

kathi roll a flatbread wrap filled with a kathi kebab, which is meat grilled on a skewer.

keema minced or ground meat, may be either chicken or goat.

keep for cover and set aside to set or develop for a prescribed duration.

khamiri fermented

khira cucumber

L

laccha long, thin slices, like shreds.

lehsun garlic

M

makki maize or corn

mandua ragi or finger millet

matra dried peas

mattar peas

meetha sweet

methi fenugreek

mooli daikon

N

nariyal coconut

nimbu lemon

P

pakke ripe

paneer Indian cottage cheese made by curdling milk.

pakoras fritters

palak spinach

panch phoran a combination of five types of whole seeds—black mustard, nigella, fenugreek, fennel and cumin.

Partition the division of the country into India and Pakistan at the time of independence from the British in 1947.

pudina mint

phulka one of the many names for the roti, chapati, rotli, and poli, among others. Generally, a phulka is small—sometimes no bigger than the palm of the hand—and thin and light.

pyaaz onion

R

raita yogurt mixed with vegetables or greens, served as an accompaniment to Indian food.

raw mango powder a souring agent.

S

saag leafy greens such as spinach and fenugreek.

samosa a triangular, deep-fried pastry case filled with savory vegetables or meat.

sarson mustard

sattu originally the flour of a combination of seven grains and lentils (*saat anaj*), corn, barley, chickpeas, green gram, pigeon peas, green peas, and horse gram, but now usually only chickpea flour.

Sindhi from Sind, a province in Pakistan and also the people of Sind, many of whom migrated to India after Partition.

T

tamatar tomato

Y

yogurt semisolid dairy product produced by the bacterial fermentation of milk.

Z

zeera cumin

Index

R

ragi atta (finger millet flour) 16, 44, 45

raisins 182

raita 20

    Aloo 60

    Boondi 167

    Gajar 84

    Pyaaz–Tamatar 102

red chili

    powder 43, 45, 46, 54, 56, 57, 59, 60, 61,
        65, 88, 92, 94, 95, 98, 102, 129, 131,
        133, 158, 167, 171, 172, 177

    whole (chile) 47

S

saffron 144

sesame seeds 84, 127

singhara atta (water-chestnut flour) 16,
    153, 168

sooji (semolina) 16, 138, 176

spinach 46, 62, 171

spring onions 84

star fruit (kamrak) 61

T

tomato 34, 54, 62, 81,138

U

urad chilka flour (black gram flour) 65, 132

V

vinegar 21, 126

W

walnuts 99

Y

yeast 99, 125, 126, 127, 129, 130, 131, 137

yogurt 20, 24, 60, 84, 102, 167

Acknowledgments

About the author

Anuradha Ravindranath was born and raised in Delhi. She inherited her interest in cooking from her late father, Ranjit Rai, who authored *Curry Curry Curry* (Penguin, 1989). This led her to write and publish *Tandoor, the Great Indian Barbecue* (Penguin, 1996) under his name, after his passing away. Her book *The Rice Cookbook—101 Simple Recipes* (Penguin, 2009) won the Gourmand World Cookbook Award for the best single subject cookbook from India. Anuradha enjoys sharing her love for cooking with enthusiasts of all ages. She has conducted cooking classes for children aged 8 to 12 years for more than 10 years, from 1995 to 2005. She has developed a concept she calls "Survival Cooking" especially for young adults planning to leave home. Her other programs include workshops, demonstrations, and hands-on experience for international groups with an interest in Indian cuisine; customized visits to local spice, fruit, and vegetable markets; workshops on "De-Stress through Cooking"; and cookery demonstrations for schools, colleges, and for cultural activities. Anuradha's other lifelong passion has been an enthusiasm and appreciation of pottery.

Author's acknowledgments

I would like to thank MadhuMadhavi Singh, who read the first draft of this book and encouraged me to get it published. Subsequently, she has been a pillar of support and patience, editing it several times until we arrived at the final text. My sincere thanks to the DK team—Aparna Sharma, who encouraged and supported my effort from the start, Neha Ahuja and Devika Awasthi for the wonderful design, and Chitra Subramanyam and Vatsal Verma for editorial support. I would also like to thank Adhyayan Sahay for bringing the recipes alive and Saumya Gupta for the beautiful photographs.

Special thanks to my husband and daughters, for whom I cooked, and extended and diversified my love for cooking, to my sons-in-law who appreciate everything I put on the dining table, and to my grand-daughters who have brought me so much joy.

Publisher's acknowledgments

The publisher would like to thank Nicobar Design for the tableware and pottery used in the photographs on pages 64, 78—79, 90—91, 101, 103, 134—135, 140—141, 142, 160—161, 166, 170, 178—179; Chandrima Banerjee for editorial input and assistance during the early stages of the book-making process; Shahid Qureshi for editorial support; Shipra Jain, Arshti Narang, and Diya Varma for design support; Harish Aggarwal and Suhita Dharamjit for support in jacket design; Raman Panwar for DTP support; Manpreet Kaur for picture research adminstration support; Shubhdeep Kaur for assistance in photography; and Tathagata Mandal for proofreading.

Resources

The publisher would like to thank the following for their kind permission to reproduce their photographs:

(Key: a-above; b-below/bottom; c-centre; f-far; l-left; r-right; t-top)

8-14 Anuradha Ravindranath. 16-17 Dorling Kindersley: Shubhdeep Kaur. 30 Dreamstime.com: Bbgum3 (b); Katkaterinara (t). 35 Dreamstime.com: Sandhyaskitchen. 80 Getty Images: IndiaPix / IndiaPicture. 86 Alamy Stock Photo: Sameer Chogale. 111 Dreamstime.com: Raj Kumar. 116-117 Dreamstime.com: Kampol Jongmeesuk. 122-123 Dorling Kindersley: Shubhdeep Kaur. 128 Shutterstock.com: Hashem Issam Alshanableh. 149 Dorling Kindersley: Shubhdeep Kaur. 150-151 Dorling Kindersley: Shubhdeep Kaur. 152 Alamy Stock Photo: Connect Images / Victoria Zeffert. 154-155 Getty Images / iStock: mtreasure. 156-157 Alamy Stock Photo: Photosindia. 164-165 Dorling Kindersley: Shubhdeep Kaur. 174-175 Dorling Kindersley: Shubhdeep Kaur

Disclaimer

Every effort has been made to acknowledge those individuals, organizations, and corporations that have helped with this book and to trace copyright holders. DK apologizes in advance if any omission has occurred. If an omission does come to light, DK will be pleased to insert the appropriate acknowledgment in the subsequent editions of the book.

Ingredients
Gandhi Foods
www.gandhifood.com

Ingredients and equipment
Desiclik
www.desiclik.com

Distacart
www.distacart.com

iShopIndian
www.ishopindian.com

Spices
The Spice House
www.thespicehouse.com

NY Spice Shop
www.nyspiceshop.com

Consulting Editor MadhuMadhavi Singh
Project Editor Vatsal Verma
Senior Editor Suefa Lee
US Editor Sharon Lucas
US Executive Editor Lori Hand
Senior Art Editor Devika Awasthi
Photography Saumya Gupta
Styling Adhyayan Sahay
Jacket Designer Vidushi Chaudhry
DTP Designer Ashok Kumar
DTP Coordinator Tarun Sharma
Pre-Production Manager Balwant Singh
Production Manager Pankaj Sharma
Managing Editor Chitra Subramanyam
Managing Art Editor Neha Ahuja Chowdhry
Consulting Publisher Aparna Sharma

Additional editorial support Rohan Sinha

First American Edition, 2025
Published in the United States by DK Publishing,
a division of Penguin Random House LLC
1745 Broadway, 20th Floor, New York, NY 10019

A catalog record for this book
is available from the Library of Congress.
ISBN: 978-0-5939-6932-8

Printed and bound in China

www.dk.com